FORMER
SOVIET
REPUBLICS

ARMENIA

AZERBAIJAN

GEORGIA

THE TRANSCAUCASUS

BY THOMAS STREISSGUTH

LUCENT BOOKS
P.O. BOX 289011
SAN DIEGO, CA 92198-9011

TITLES IN THE FORMER SOVIET REPUBLICS SERIES INCLUDE:

The Baltics
The Central Asian States
The Russian Federation
The Transcaucasus
Ukraine

Library of Congress Cataloging-in-Publication Data

Streissguth, Thomas, 1965–
    The Transcaucasus / by Thomas Streissguth.
        p. cm. — (Modern nations of the world)
    Includes bibliographical references and index.
    ISBN 1-56006-736-5
    1. Transcaucasia—History—Juvenile literature. [1. Georgia (Republic)
2. Armenia (Republic) 3. Azerbaijan.] I. Title. II. Series.
    DK509 .G56 2001
    947.5—dc21

                                00-012186

Copyright © 2001 by Lucent Books, Inc.
P.O. Box 289011, San Diego, CA 92198-9011
Printed in the U.S.A.

CONTENTS

FOREWORD

THE CURTAIN RISES

Through most of the last century, the world was widely perceived as divided into two realms separated by what British prime minister Winston Churchill once called the "iron curtain." This curtain was, of course, not really made of iron, but of ideas and values. Countries to the west of this symbolic curtain, including the United States, were democracies founded upon the economic principles of capitalism. To the east, in the Soviet Union, a new social and economic order known as communism prevailed. The United States and the Soviet Union were locked for much of the twentieth century in a struggle for military, economic, and political dominance around the world.

But the Soviet Union could not sustain its own weight, burdened as it was by a hugely inefficient centralized government bureaucracy, by long-term neglect of domestic needs in favor of spending untold billions on the military, and by the systematic repression of thought and expression among its citizens. For years the military and internal police apparatus had held together the Soviet Union's diverse peoples. But even these entities could not overcome the corruption, the inefficiency, and the inability of the Communist system to provide the basic necessities for the Soviet people.

The unrest that signaled the beginning of the end for the Soviet Union began in the satellite countries of Eastern Europe in 1988—in East Germany, followed by Hungary, and Poland. By 1990, the independence movement had moved closer to the Soviet heartland. Lithuania became the first Baltic nation to declare its independence. By December 1991, all fifteen union republics—Armenia, Azerbaijan, Belarus, Estonia, Georgia, Kazakhstan, Kyrgyzstan, Latvia, Lithuania, Moldova, Russia, Tajikistan, Turkmenistan, Ukraine, Uzbekistan—had done the same. The Soviet Union had officially ceased to exist.

Today the people of new nations such as Uzbekistan, Latvia, Belarus, Georgia, Ukraine, and Russia itself (still the largest nation on earth) must deal with the loss of the certainties of the Soviet era and face the new economic and social challenges of the present. The fact that many of these regions have little if any history of self-governance adds to the problem. For better or worse, many social problems were kept in check by a powerful government during the Soviet era, and long-standing cultural, ethnic, and other tensions are once again threatening to tear apart these new and fragile nations. Whether these regions make an effective transition to a market economy based on capitalism and resolve their internal economic crises by becoming vital and successful participants in world trade; whether their social crises push them back in the direction of dictatorship or civil war, or move them toward greater political, ethnic, and religious tolerance; and perhaps most important of all, whether average citizens can come to believe in their own ability to improve their lives and their own power to create a government and a nation of laws that works in their own best

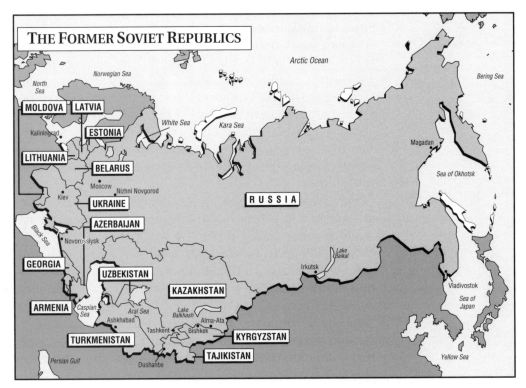

THE FORMER SOVIET REPUBLICS

interests, are questions that the entire world, not just former Soviet citizens are pondering.

Sociologists and political scientists alike point to instability in the former Soviet republics as a serious threat to world peace and the balance of global power, and therefore it is more important than ever to be accurately informed about this politically and economically critical part of the world. With Modern Nations: Former Soviet Republics, Lucent Books provides information about the people and recent history of the former Soviet republics, with an emphasis on those aspects of their culture, history, and current situation that seem most likely to play a role in the future course of each of these new nations emerging from the shadows of the now vanished iron curtain.

INTRODUCTION

TROUBLE AT THE CROSSROADS

In the southern part of what once was the Soviet Union, between the Black Sea and the Caspian Sea, begins the Transcaucasus, a region divided into the three nations of Armenia, Azerbaijan, and Georgia. Though these countries cover a small geographical area, historically they have held an importance out of proportion to their size. The Caucasus Mountains, and the valleys and plains that lie in their shadows, figure in some of the oldest myths in human memory. Armies came and went as more powerful nations attempted to conquer and control the region's abundant natural resources. In the eighteenth and nineteenth centuries, Transcaucasia became a central prize in what was known as "The Great Game," a contest between Russia, the Ottoman Empire, and Great Britain for control of central Asia and of the strategic crossroads between Europe, Asia, and the Middle East.

After Soviet rule began in the 1920s, the Transcaucasus countries joined the world's largest socialist state—a new kind of empire, founded on the principle that all goods should be held in common, that one political party and its members should govern, and that every individual should work, live, and play in the service of the state and the Communist Party. But Soviet rule did not sit well with the individualistic ethnic groups of the Caucasus, who valued their independence and self-sufficiency above all. Several of the first open revolts against Soviet rule occurred in the Transcaucasus, and in 1991 these small nations placed themselves at the front of the line as the Soviet republics prepared to exit the short-lived empire.

In 1995 all of the Transcaucasus republics adopted new constitutions, formally declaring their independence from the precepts and structures of one-party rule. Market economics, rather than central planning and state ownership, were declared the new guiding principles of the region's economic life. The Soviet constitution was a thing of the past, but the Soviet legacy remained: economic disaster, in which obsolete industries operated at a loss, everyday goods were in short supply, and low wages barely fed the individual worker.

The situation was familiar in all of the former Soviet republics, particularly in Russia, the home of the Communist revolution. Yet in the Transcaucasus an additional disaster unfolded: ethnic feuding that hindered the economic recovery and threatened to turn the Transcaucasus into a patchwork of squabbling clans and ministates. While the government of Georgia dealt with three separatist movements, Azerbaijan lost control of an entire region in which ethnic Azerbaijanis are outnumbered by ethnic Armenians. Meanwhile, a strangling economic blockade of landlocked Armenia by Azerbaijan

forced the emigration of the most skilled and educated Armenians, many of whom left their homeland just to survive.

To outside observers, these difficult problems seemed all but unsolvable, especially in light of widespread corruption among political leaders and parties. Independence has proven hard, but the people of the Transcaucasus have long experience with hardships and conflict. The nations of the Transcaucasus can still rely on their important natural resources, and their strategic location as a trading crossroads, to draw themselves up from and out of the past.

A dirt road stretches through the foothills of the Caucasus Mountains in Georgia.

1

MOUNTAINS AND CROSSROADS

Looking south, toward Asia, from the plains of southern Russia, the Caucasus Mountains rise in a distant haze, towering over the landscape like the wall of an immense natural fortress. The Transcaucasus nations of Georgia, Armenia, and Azerbaijan lie within this mountain fastness, astride a crossroads between the Caspian and Black Seas that links Eastern Europe to the Middle East and Asia. The Transcaucasus is one of the oldest continuously inhabited regions in human history, and has been a source of inspiration and fascination for millennia. To the ancient Greeks and Mesopotamians, the Caucasus was the land of gods and mythical beasts; to traders and explorers, it was home to fierce nomadic tribes who harried visitors from the backs of their swift and semiwild horses. The natural wonders in this forbidding territory were even more awe-inspiring, as historian Robert Bedrosian notes:

> During the third through first millenia B.C. . . . Eastern Asia Minor differed in important ways from its modern incarnation. First, many now-extinct or dormant volcanoes were then active. The two Ararats, Nemrut, Suphan, Rewanduz, and Savalan were among the more prominent volcanoes spewing molten lava and rocks into the night sky, surely stimulating the awe and imaginations of observers. Second, the flora and fauna were richer. . . . Herds of wild elephants roamed in the Van-Urmiah area and as far west as the Euphrates river, while . . . there was a profusion of types of birds, fish, bears, and mountain cats no longer found there. [1]

The Transcaucasus has long been a scene of conflict as well. Ancient Roman, Macedonian, and Persian armies arrived to do battle in these rugged mountain passes. In later centuries, Ottoman Turks and Russians fought over the Transcaucasus in a bitter contest over economic, religious, and cultural influence. In both ancient and modern times, natural resources have also attracted foreign attention. One writer notes that the Transcaucasus has "almost always assumed a value far greater than the silks and spices, and latterly the oil and mines, which it possesses. Its awkward position on the invasion and trade paths between two continents has determined its eventful history."[2]

THE THREE NATIONS OF THE TRANSCAUCASUS

Armenia, with an area of about 11,500 square miles, is the smallest of the Transcaucasus nations. This nation, about the size of the state of Maryland, lies south of Georgia and west of Azerbaijan. Armenia's western border abuts Turkey, which also has a sizable population of ethnic Armenians. A narrow corridor reaches south and links Armenia and Iran. Armenia also borders an unusual enclave known as Naxçivan, which forms an island of Azerbaijani territory lying between southern Armenia and northwestern Iran.

A rugged region of mountains and steep valleys known as the Armenian Plateau crosses Armenia, linking the Caucasus and the hills of northeastern Turkey. The plateau is cut by the Araks River, a waterway that forms Armenia's borders with Iran and with Turkey, where it is known as the Aras. Supplied by several short mountain rivers, Lake Sevan in turn feeds the Razdan

River, a tributary of the Araks. The lake serves Armenians as an important source of fresh water for irrigation and as a source of hydropower.

The average elevation in this mountainous nation is 5,600 feet—over a mile above sea level. A legacy of the region's volcanic history is the fact that nearly all of Armenia is seismically active, and strong earthquakes are common. There is abundant volcanic surface rock, and the rich soil created as this rock breaks down is home to more than 3,200 different species of plants and trees.

Although mountains and rocky highlands dominate the map of Armenia, the Armenians have been productive farmers throughout their history. In the plateau surrounding the capital of Yerevan, small farms produce fruits, vegetables, and cereal grains, which are sold in the street markets of Armenia's cities. Grapes grown on the steep hillsides supply the Armenian winemaking industry, long a mainstay of the nation's economy. Armenians also grow cotton to supply textile and carpet factories.

Mountains and rocky highlands dominate the Armenian landscape.

Lying north and east of Armenia is Azerbaijan, the largest of the Transcaucasus nations, covering about 33,400 square miles between the eastern ranges of the Caucasus Mountains and the shores of the Caspian Sea. Across the northern border of Azerbaijan is a region of the Russian Republic known as Dagestan, and the southeastern limits of Georgia. To the west, across the Lesser Caucasus Mountains, begins Armenia, and to the south across the Araks River and the Talysh Mountains is Iran. The highlands of southern Azerbaijan include the region of Nagorno-Karabakh, an enclave within Azerbaijan that is dominated by ethnic Armenians and is the object of a long-standing feud between the governments of Armenia and Azerbaijan.

Generally, the farther east one travels in Azerbaijan, the lower the elevation and the more level the landscape. Crossing this country from west to east is the Kura River, the country's principal waterway, which empties into the Caspian Sea. A dam along the Kura at the town of Mingaçevir created the Mingaçevir Reservoir, a principal source of fresh water in a sometimes drought-stricken country. The Mingaçevir and a series of small rivers irrigate the Kura Lowlands, where farmers grow cereal grains such as barley, oats, and wheat. Azeri farms also produce fruits—peaches, grapes, pears, and pomegranates.

The Kura River (pictured) flows through the Georgian capital of Tbilisi.

Although its produce is much prized, particularly in Russia and the other former Soviet republics to the north, Azerbaijan's most important natural resources are the crude oil and natural gas found in wells on the bottom of the Caspian Sea. The plentiful and valuable energy resources have been an economic blessing, as well as an environmental curse. Azerbaijan, which began commercial oil production more than one hundred years ago, can still rely on oil to bring in money for the nation's treasury and provide jobs. But the wells and pumping equipment that line the shores of what is essentially a large lake have made the western Caspian one of the world's most polluted bodies of water.

Slightly larger than the state of South Carolina, Georgia covers 26,900 square miles between the Black Sea and the southern limit of the Caucasus Mountains. Although not as large as Azerbaijan, Georgia is home to a diverse terrain. Elevations exceed 15,000 feet at several points in the Greater Caucasus Mountains, which run parallel to Georgia's long border with

Russia, from the Georgian province of Abkhazia (which considers itself an autonomous republic though its 1992 declaration of independence was rejected by Georgia) in the northwest to the border with Azerbaijan in the southeast. A series of fast-flowing rivers, including the Kodori, the Inguri, and the Rioni flow from the north to the southwest, and from the mountain highlands to the Colchis Lowlands, a flat triangle of land that once formed the bottom of the Black Sea. The principal cities of this western region are Kutaisi, on the Rioni River, and the Black Sea ports of Sukhumi and Batumi.

Crossing the middle of Georgia are the Suram Mountains, the source of the Kura River. After it descends from these highlands, the Kura flows through the center of Tbilisi, the capital of Georgia. Tbilisi is one of several busy urban centers that lie within the Kartalinian Plain, a fertile and well-watered region that produces a wide variety of fruit, vegetable, and cereal crops. Farther east are the smaller valleys of the Iori and Alazani Rivers. In the west—the warmest region of the country—valuable cash crops such as tea, tobacco, and flowers (used in the making of perfume) are grown for export. Georgia also produces a wide variety of citrus, such as oranges and lemons, and hundreds of varieties of grapes. In well-watered areas, silkworms are raised on the leaves of mulberry trees.

Georgia borders Turkey and Armenia in the south and Azerbaijan to the southeast. Because the Caucasus Mountains to the north form an obstacle to trade, the few roads that pass through Georgia to Russia have long been essential to Armenian and

Azerbaijani traders and merchants. Georgia is also the only nation of the Transcaucasus with access to an international water route via the Black Sea, which links the republic to the Mediterranean Sea. Pleasant resort towns share the Black Sea coast with ports where manufactured goods, crude oil, and agricultural produce are shipped from the Transcaucasus to countries around the world.

ETHNIC GROUPS AND CONFLICTS IN THE TRANSCAUCASUS

Over the centuries, its position as a strategic crossroads has also made the Transcaucasus a roiling cauldron of peoples, languages, and cultures. Each of the three Transcaucasus countries still includes sizable ethnic minorities related to cultures of neighboring nations. Although during the Soviet era the government managed to keep ethnic conflicts under control, the crumbling of Soviet control in the early 1990s sparked renewed violence in the region. Armenians, Azerbaijanis, and Georgians advanced competing demands for land and natural resources, while smaller ethnic groups demanded freedoms that had been denied to them under Soviet rule.

In part because of historic rivalries in the region, the Transcaucasus countries suffered bitter ethnic warfare at the dawn of their independence in the early 1990s. For example, most ethnic Azerbaijanis fled Armenia between 1988 and 1992, a period of bloody confrontations between Azerbaijanis and Armenians. The same conflict led to a mass exodus of Armenians from Azerbaijan. (Ethnically, modern Armenia is the least diverse country of the Transcaucasus. About 95 percent of all the people living within Armenia's borders are culturally Armenian, although they live with small minorities of Azerbaijanis, who generally live in the eastern half of the country, and an even smaller number of ethnic Russians, who arrived when Armenia was a part of the Soviet Union.)

Across the northern border, Russian, Armenian, Azerbaijani, Ajarian, Ossetian, and Abkhazian minorities inhabit Georgia, where smaller ethnic groups such as the Mingrelians have distinct traditions and dialects of their own. Georgia has an ethnic composition of nearly 9 percent Armenian, 6 percent Russian, 6 percent Ajarian, and 5 percent ethnic Azerbaijani. Smaller minority groups include the Svanetians (also known as the Svens), the Mingrelians, and the Laz.

THE ABKHAZIANS OF GEORGIA

Abkhazia, an autonomous republic of Georgia, has a population of about five hundred thousand. The Ottoman Empire ruled Abkhazia for over two centuries, starting in the sixteenth century. Although the Turkish rulers introduced the Islamic religion, the numbers of Christians and Muslims in modern Abkhazia is roughly equal. A more widespread legacy of Turkish rule is the distinctive and complex Abkhazian language. This Turkish dialect, a member of the Northwest Caucasian language group, has fifty-six consonants and only two vowels.

Turkish rule of Abkhazia continued until the Russians forced the Turks from northern Georgia and turned Abkhazia into a Russian protectorate in 1864. In March 1921, three and a half years after the Communist revolution, the Red Army seized all of Georgia and made Abkhazia an independent republic. Abkhazia then formally became part of Georgia but retained its status as a Soviet republic until 1931.

In 1978, Abkhazians launched an unsuccessful campaign for secession from Georgia and incorporation into the Russian Federation. Twelve years later, when the Soviet Union began to break up, the Abkhazian regional parliament declared its independence from Georgia. The Abkhazian government adopted the 1925 Abkhazian constitution that designated Abkhazia a sovereign state.

Prior to the conflict with Georgia, native Abkhazians constituted only 17.8 percent of the republic's population, with ethnic Georgians comprising 45.7 percent, Russians 16 percent, and Armenians 15 percent. The republic, which lies along Georgia's northern border with Russia, remains a primarily agricultural region that produces tobacco, tea, silk, and various fruit crops. Abkhazian industries include timber, textiles, and shoe manufacturing.

Georgian soldiers inspect their weapons during the conflict in Abkhazia.

The Abkhazians and Ossetians constitute 2 and 3 percent of the Georgian mosaic, respectively. The Ajarians, though a distinct ethnographic group, remain Georgians and speak a Georgian dialect. They number about one hundred thousand and live along the southwestern Georgian border with Turkey.

Ethnic diversity may be even greater in Azerbaijan, which is home to distinct ethnic groups in the Lezgins, Avars, Talysh, and Kurds. The nation's unity is, as a result, under stress. For example, the Lezgin people of northern Azerbaijan have sought to unite with their ethnic kin across the border in Russia, where large numbers of Lezgins live in the semi-independent region of Dagestan. The active separatist movement Sadval advocates unification with neighboring Dagestan in the Russian Federation.

Sizable ethnic groups such as the Talysh are culturally aligned with other nations as well. According to various estimates, the number of Talysh ranges between twenty-one thousand and two hundred thousand people. The Talysh, who are related to the Iranians, live in southern Azerbaijan near the country's border with Iran. Such cultural mixed allegiances work both ways: The 13 million ethnic Azerbaijanis who live in Iran are more closely related to native Azerbaijanis than to the Talysh or to other Iranians.

The mosaic of ethnic groups within Azerbaijan, and in the Transcaucasus in general, dates back nearly four millenia. The first settlers of the lowlands of Azerbaijan came from the Caucasus Mountains. These Caucasic people began intermarrying with invaders who arrived from the south, from ancient Persia. The inhabitants of Azerbaijan later mixed with the Seljuk Turks, who arrived in the eleventh century A.D. In the process of repeated invasions, ethnic intermarriage, and subsequent division of the region between competing great powers, smaller groups of people sharing a common culture and dialect formed themselves into distinctive communities that inhabited their own well-defined territories irrespective of national boundaries. Added to this volatile mix has been the spark of differing religious faiths, which continues to touch off conflicts great and small within the Transcaucasus.

TROUBLE AT THE CROSSROADS

The region known as the Transcaucasus has enjoyed an important place in history mainly due to its geographic location as a crossroads between East and West. Thanks to their location, the three countries of this region share a common history, at times a history of prosperity and achievement but also a history of defeat and hardship under the rule of the different empires and invaders. As one expert has noted of the Transcaucasus region, "A strategic location at the meeting point of empires, tempting economic resources and trade routes, and openness to the passage of armies as well as merchants' caravans have combined to keep the region fragmented and to make it a favorite battleground for neighboring powers."[3]

In the past, the mountains served as a natural fortress for the people of the Transcaucasus, and the terrain is still famous for its role in their successful defense against the invading armies of the Persian Empire. But the rugged terrain had another important effect: By preventing easy travel and communication, it hindered the development of large, cohesive societies. The people of the Transcaucasus have always been sharply divided by culture, by language, and by religion. The many clans, ethnic groups, and rival social classes have made this one of the most discordant and turbulent regions on earth.

For outsiders, the Transcaucasus could not be ignored; the region held great wealth in the form of valuable mineral resources,

THE FIGHT OVER NAGORNO-KARABAKH

One of the worst ethnic conflicts in the modern Transcaucasus began in the late 1980s, when fighting began between Armenia and Azerbaijan over the small enclave known as Nagorno-Karabakh. This region lies entirely within Azerbaijan, but is home to an Armenian majority, which demanded self-rule and independence from the control of the Azerbaijan government in Baku. Before this war broke out, there were more than four hundred thousand Armenians living in Azerbaijan. The bitter fighting and migration on a massive scale, however, left only a few Armenians behind.

The legacy of the fight over Nagorno-Karabakh continues into the twenty-first century. To retaliate for Armenian shelling of Azerbaijani villages, Azerbaijan placed a blockade that prevents food, fuel, and other vital supplies from reaching Armenia. This blockade has done severe economic damage to Armenia, cutting the country off from outside trade and from much-needed foreign investment and assistance.

fertile valleys, and hardwood forests. As a result, the peoples of the Transcaucasus have experienced long and hard periods of dominance by foreign powers. Invasion by outsiders was not the only source of conflict for the Transcaucasus nations. As often as they have cooperated, these countries have fought among themselves over land, over water, and over their limited resources—a fight that continues as the twenty-first century begins.

THE CONQUESTS OF
THE TRANSCAUCASUS

Throughout its recorded history, the Transcaucasus has en-
dured invasions and foreign conquests. Nomadic peoples including the Scythians and the Cimmerians, who first settled
north and east of the Black Sea, drove through the Caucasus
Mountains in search of valuable minerals, good hunting, and
fertile land. In the eighth century B.C., the Medes pushed north
from their homeland in northern Persia (modern Iran) and
built a state that reached the western shores of the Caspian Sea.
At the same time, Greek traders were building small ports along
the southern Black Sea shores, from which Greek religion and
culture spread into the Transcaucasus. Persian armies arrived
in the sixth century B.C. under Cyrus the Great, the first king of
the Achaemenid dynasty. For two centuries, while satraps loyal
to the Achaemenids ruled their cities and land, the Persians
and Greeks fought for influence and control of resources in the
Transcaucasus.

The contest reached its climax in the campaigns of Alexander
the Great, a skilled young Macedonian general who defeated
the Persians at the decisive Battle of Arbela. This victory allowed
Alexander's successors to appoint the governors of ancient Armenia, a territory that at the time covered the southern Transcaucasus as well as eastern Asia Minor. But Alexander's death
without an heir in 323 B.C. turned his Macedonian empire into
a collection of smaller states ruled by squabbling Macedonian
generals. These states could offer little resistance to the armies
of Rome. Around 190 B.C., the legions of Rome arrived in Asia
Minor. The Romans overthrew the independent states in the region and established satrapies of their own under two obedient
governors, Artaxias and Zariadres, in the southern Caucasus
and ancient Armenia.

The rise of the Roman Empire allowed the Armenians to
turn autonomy into true independence. Under King Tigran II,

At the Battle of Arbela, Alexander the Great and his army wrested control of the Transcaucasus from the Persians.

who allied himself to the Romans, the Armenians established a large state that extended from the Caspian Sea south to the Mediterranean. Armenian independence ended in 30 B.C., however, when Roman legions invaded. Less than one hundred years later, in A.D. 62, troops from the Persian province of Parthia defeated the legions and ended the Roman monopoly. For the next three centuries, the Romans and Persians contested the region, until an agreement in 387 divided ancient Armenia between the two empires.

RELIGION AND CULTURE IN THE TRANSCAUCASUS

By this time, Christianity was the officially accepted faith in Armenia, the first nation on earth to elevate this relatively new religion to such a status. In the fifth century, the Armenians invented their unique alphabet and translated much of the Old and New Testaments into their own language. But the acceptance of Christianity also ensured a long-standing conflict with the Persians. Centuries later, the coming of Islam to nations to the south and east further isolated Armenia from its neighbors.

For Georgia, the enduring influence of invaders has also been most evident in religion. Until about A.D. 330, when Georgia formally adopted Christianity, many of its people were followers of the ancient fire-worshiping religion of Persia.

In the easternmost stretches of the Transcaucasus, Christianity did not take hold. Instead the people of Azerbaijan took from later Arab and Turkish conquerors their cultural, linguistic, and religious traditions.

The Arab conquest of the Transcaucasus proved much briefer than the rule of the Persians or Romans. Yet the Arab conquest left an enduring legacy—in Azerbaijan, in particular—in the form of Islam. Brought at the head of powerful armies, Islam combined secular administration and religious belief into a single, all-encompassing authority. This religion emphasized community among believers and was aggressively introduced throughout all of Azerbaijan, although it met stiff resistance

The Arab conquest of the Transcaucasus brought Islam to Azerbaijan.

from the stronger Christian communities in Armenia and Georgia. Azerbaijan was ruled by powerful local elites, who grew wealthy from a busy trade in carpets, ceramics, leather goods, and other merchandise. After three centuries of Arab rule, only Azerbaijan remained Islamic, although there were, and still are, Islamic followers in Georgia as well.

THE TURKISH CONQUEST

The Seljuk Turks, a people originally from the steppes of central Asia, swept into the Transcaucasus not long after the Arab conquest, defeating Armenia at the Battle of Manzikert in 1071. The Seljuks introduced the Turkish language and customs, and through intermarriage created a new branch of Turkic society in the Transcaucasus.

The Transcaucasus, meanwhile, still attracted other foreigners who were drawn to the region's natural resources. Even as early as the thirteenth century, the Italian adventurer Marco Polo arrived at the shores of the Caspian, where he described a curious natural phenomenon known in the region for millenia:

> On the confines toward Georgine there is a fountain from which oil springs in great abundance, inasmuch as a hundred shiploads might be taken from it at one time. This oil is not good to use with food, but 'tis good to burn, and is also used to anoint camels that have the mange. People come from vast distances to fetch it, for in all countries round there is no other oil. [4]

The strongest foreign influence in the Transcaucasus came not with Europeans, with Christianity, or even with the Seljuk Turks, but with the Ottoman Turks, who arrived in the fifteenth century. Followers of Islam, they also brought a strong foundation for Turkish rule and culture in the form of language. As Shireen Hunter notes, "The Turkic peoples left one lasting and extremely important legacy—namely their language—which ever since has affected the region's cultural and political development." [5] After the Ottoman Turkish conquest, many people of the Transcaucasus began to see themselves as Turks.

Turkish influence in Azerbaijan was at first strongest among the most educated of Azerbaijani society. Although nearly all Azerbaijanis called themselves "Turks," or similar terms (such as Tatar), the way Turkish culture was expressed was unique. As one history of Azerbaijan notes, "Most Azerbaijani intelligentsia

recognized their identity as Turks but worked consciously to build a Turkish identity that was particularly Azerbaijani."[6] Turkish language, music, and literature soon became very popular in Azerbaijan, and much of modern Azerbaijani culture is rooted in Turkish influence.

The Turkish sultans extended their control of the Transcaucasus through a distinct form of government, in which religious leaders were given wide-ranging authority over their communities. Local governors, or viziers, were responsible for keeping the peace, dispensing justice, and collecting the sultan's annual tribute in gold and trade goods. The Muslim house of prayer, known as the mosque, appeared in cities and villages throughout the region. While earlier rulers had focused on control of trade and resources, the Ottoman rulers allowed conquered territories some independence in matters of law and

In the fifteenth century, the Ottoman Turks conquered the Transcaucasus where they had a profound influence over politics and culture.

religion. As a world power, which dealt with the wealthy European powers on an equal footing, the Turks also provided the people of the Transcaucasus, and especially the people of Azerbaijan, an avenue to higher education and greater economic opportunity.

Turkish influence was not limited to Azerbaijan, however. The Turks were also present in Georgia, leaving behind a small ethnic Georgian minority group known as the Ajarians. Despite centuries of living in predominantly Christian Georgia, the Ajarians would remain Muslim through the twentieth century. Another important ethnic minority, the Abkhazians, stand in contrast to the Ajarians, however. Although they adopted a Turkic language, the Abkhazians were more strongly influenced by the Christian Georgians, so there is no strong Islamic identity among the Abkhazians. There are no mosques in Abkhazia today, and as an expert on the region stresses, "They are currently about equally divided between Orthodox Christians and Moslems."[7]

RUSSIA AND THE TRANSCAUCASUS

Ottoman Turks and Persians shared control over the Transcaucasus region for much of the sixteenth through the eighteenth centuries. The late eighteenth century, however, saw the arrival of a power from north of the Caucasus: the armies of the Russian czar, who annexed part of Georgia in 1801 and eventually extended Russian control to the entire country. Later, after defeating the Persians on the battlefield, the Russians imposed the Treaty of Turkmanchay in 1828, which made what today is Armenia a province of the Russian Empire. Russians and Ottoman Turks would, however, continue to compete over the Transcaucasus. Although Russia would either claim title outright or try to influence the nations of the Transcaucasus, the Turks would continue to play an important role in the region, particularly in Azerbaijan.

For the most part, the people of the Transcaucasus welcomed Russian control, although there was resistance in Azerbaijan, where the influence of the Ottoman Turks and of Islam was much greater than in Armenia or Georgia. While the Islamic Azerbaijanis saw the Orthodox Christian Russians as a threat to their way of life, the Christian nations of Armenia and Georgia were more accepting of Russian rule. There was also a perception among the Georgians and Armenians that Russia provided them with protection from the Turks, a factor that contributed to the growing rift between Armenia and Georgia on the one side, and Azerbaijan on the other.

Russia also tended to foster other divisions between the Armenians and Georgians, as the Russian czars sought to better control the Transcaucasus by setting one ethnic group against another. They accomplished this by routinely favoring one region in economic development, another in the building of roads and public buildings, and so forth. As Russian favor shifted back and forth, resentment between Armenians and Georgians grew.

Another important factor that kept Armenia, Azerbaijan, and Georgia firmly in the Russian orbit was the nineteenth-century doctrine of socialism, which appealed for different reasons to people in each of the three countries. In Georgia, for example, socialism attracted farmers who saw their country's most productive lands being held by a small clique of landowning families. Many Georgian farmers, most of whom were slavelike serfs or impoverished tenant farmers, supported the socialist demand for collective ownership of property. For Armenians, on

Arriving during the late eighteenth century, Russian armies were not always peacefully welcomed by the people of the Transcaucasus.

THE EVERLASTING FIRE OF ANCIENT BAKU

Oil was not a modern discovery on the western shores of the Caspian Sea. From ancient times, the burning brimstone of Baku, also known as the "Everlasting Fire," was legendary among European and Asian travelers. The British writer John Hanway wrote the following account in *An Account of British Trade over the Caspian Sea* in 1754. It is taken from Sylvia Volk's article, "The Fire-Temple at Baku."

The Everlasting Fire lies about ten miles NE by E off the city of Baku, on a dry rocky land; there are several ancient stone temples there, including one small temple at which 40 or 50 Indian pilgrims may usually be seen. Near the temple is a low cleft of rock, in which is a horizontal gap—two feet from the ground, six feet long, and three feet broad—from which issues a constant flame, in color and gentleness like that of a spirit lamp only more pure; and when the wind blows, this torch rises sometimes eight feet high. On a calm day, the fire burns lower. It leaves no soot or impression on the rock. The Indians worship it, saying that it cannot be resisted, and if extinguished will only spring up in another place.

All around this place, for a distance of two miles, if one digs a mere two or three inches into the ground and applies a live coal, the uncovered soil instantly takes fire—almost before the coal touches the earth. This flame heats the soil but neither consumes nor marks it, and it is not terribly hot. This soil, if carried away, does not light or burn. The ground is dry and stony, and the stonier it is, the stronger and clearer is the flame kindled there. There is a sulphorous smell, like that of naphtha, but this is not too offensive.

One of the first oil wells to be drilled in Azerbaijan.

the other hand, the socialist movement promised an end to the corrupt and weakening Ottoman government. In Azerbaijan, socialist writers and speakers stressed equal economic opportunity, promising the Muslim Azerbaijanis an end to the years of economic domination by ethnic Armenians living in Azerbaijan.

The socialist doctrine had the effect of intensifying a growing conflict over the benefits of the oil industry in Azerbaijan. The "oil boom" in the cosmopolitan Azerbaijani capital of Baku was so significant that, according to journalist Suzanne Goldenberg, "By 1898, Baku's output had surpassed that of the entire American oil industry" and "had also produced the world's first oil tanker and the first oil pipeline, which was made of wood." [8] The emerging oil business in Azerbaijan brought large investments from foreign companies, making Azerbaijan the first country in the Transcaucasus to attract such capital. A new railway linked the boom town of Baku with Georgia's port of Batumi on the Black Sea, and thousands of workers poured into Azerbaijan to take up jobs in a burgeoning energy industry.

There was a problem, however, with this new industry. Armenians owned many of the industries in Baku, and most of the better jobs went to Armenians, Georgians, and Russians, with most Azerbaijanis holding only lower-paying manual labor jobs. This inequality caused tension between the local ethnic Armenians and Azerbaijanis and, as one historian observes, "The differences in their economic status perpetuated and accentuated barriers of culture, religion and language." [9] As historian Anahide Ter Minassian notes: "Azeri national consciousness developed not so much against the Russian colonizer as against the Armenian." [10]

Another problem was the fact that the Russian treasury, and not the Azerbaijanis, seemed to be benefiting the most from oil. The inequalities and resentment over their apparent second-class status contributed to a rising nationalism among the Azerbaijanis.

World War I and the Armenian Genocide

Internal tensions notwithstanding, the Transcaucasus was destined to be a pawn in a game played by much more powerful nations. The game grew serious in the early twentieth century, when two rival alliances were formed among the most powerful nations of Europe. On the Allied side, Russia sided with

France and Great Britain. Opposing this alliance were the Central Powers of Germany, Austria-Hungary, and the Ottoman Empire. In 1914 the assassination of an Austrian archduke in the Balkans brought about the start of World War I, a conflict that caught the Transcaucasus in a dangerous confrontation between the opposing Russian and Ottoman Turkish empires. The fate of the Armenians, Georgians, and Azerbaijanis would all depend on the course of the war and the actions of the Russians and the Turks.

In one way, the situation in the Transcaucasus mirrored that of the outside world. The Armenians and Georgians looked to Russia as their only defense against Turkish invasion. Azerbaijan, meanwhile, looked for Turkish help in overcoming Russian rule, and Ottoman leaders called for unification with Azerbaijan in a "pan-Turkic" empire.

War, when it came, brought chaos to the Transcaucasus. While the Russian armies suffered devastating defeats on the empire's western frontier, Armenians and Azeris fought pitched battles in the mountain valleys: Massacres of civilians became a common occurrence. Yet the defeats Russia was suffering convinced many leaders in the Transcaucasus that their

Armenian troops prepare to march into battle during World War I.

small states must join forces to survive at all. To strengthen their mutual defenses, Armenia, Georgia, and Azerbaijan formed the Transcaucasus Federation in 1917. Azeri leaders had decided that membership in the federation was preferable to outright rule by the Ottoman Turks, and Armenia and Georgia also hoped to discourage Turkey from military campaigns in the Transcaucasus. The Armenians and Georgians also saw the presence of Allied forces in the region as a means of guaranteeing their independence.

But in a region long wracked by national and ethnic rivalries, peace seemed as elusive as ever. His position weakened by military defeats and angry riots among urban workers, the Russian czar abdicated his throne early 1917, and a radical socialist faction known as the Bolsheviks took power in October of that year. Civil war soon engulfed what had been the Russian empire. And while Russia plunged into chaos, the people of the Transcaucasus returned to their ancient feuds.

A power vacuum developed in the Transcaucasus, which was wracked by violence as various factions attempted to seize and hold power. The three-nation Transcaucasus Federation proved brief. On May 26, 1918, Georgia declared its independence. Azerbaijan followed suit the next day, and Armenia declared its independence on May 29.

When in the fall of 1918 Germany collapsed, and the defeat of the Turks at the hands of the Allies put an end to the Ottoman Empire, the Transcaucasus was left largely to its own devices. The Allies dispatched a token force to the region in an attempt to impose order. But the Turkish refusal to abide by the terms of the postwar peace treaty, and the reluctance of the Allies to deploy troops to enforce the treaty, allowed the Turks to reimpose their dominance in the Transcaucasus.

The subsequent departure of the Allied forces left the Transcaucasus vulnerable to Turkish aggression. Each nation in the region sought to deal with Turkey in its own way. While the Azerbaijanis welcomed this resurgence of Turkish power, the Georgians sought some kind of peaceful relationship with what was now the Turkish republic. Armenian leaders, on the other hand, claiming that ethnic Armenians within the old Ottoman Empire had been subject to genocide in 1915, continued to see modernized Turkey as an implacable enemy.

Once again, the nations of the Transcaucasus were on their own, dealing with weak economies, food shortages, and foreign

Pictured is a group of Armenian refugees after they were forced by Turkish forces to flee from their homes.

aggression. For Armenia, the problems were particularly severe. As a British historian observes, the "economic conditions were catastrophic. The scenes of famine and privation in the winter of 1918–1919 were as bad as the horrors of 1915. Half a million refugees, dressed in rags or sacking, roamed the land, or shivered in caves and dugouts."[11]

Despite the hardships, all three nations could boast of important achievements. The three governments managed to hold democratic elections. All three established free primary education, and each nation passed laws providing for the welfare of the poorest citizens. Socially progressive policies were the norm in the region and some historic milestones were reached. In Armenia in 1918, universal suffrage extended the right to vote to women, two years earlier than the United States and long before many other countries of the world.

RUSSIA RETURNS TO THE TRANSCAUCASUS

These accomplishments were not enough, however, to overcome the greatest threat to peace and stability: the demand for land. Each country had at least one territorial dispute with its neighbors. Weakened by these disputes, the Transcaucasus was still vulnerable to attack—and not from Turkey this time, but from Russia.

The Russians had been preoccupied, at first by World War I, then by the revolutions of 1917, and then by civil war. After the October 1917 revolution, which brought the Bolsheviks to power, the Red (Bolshevik) Army had launched a new advance on the Transcaucasus. While the Red Army swept into the Transcaucasus in the spring of 1920, Russian Communists worked with their comrades in the cities of the Transcaucasus to stir up discontent against the established governments.

With the help of this internal agitation, the Russians forced the government of Azerbaijan to surrender in April 1920. Armenia, facing threats from Turkey as well as from Russia, ceded territory to Turkey and then surrendered to Russia for protection against further Turkish aggression. And despite a secret treaty of May 1920, in which the Bolsheviks promised to respect Georgian independence, the Red Army invaded Georgia in February 1921. For the peoples of the Transcaucasus, independence would have to wait another seventy years.

3

THE SOVIET ERA

The leaders of the Bolshevik Revolution established their capital in Moscow and founded the Union of Soviet Socialist Republics (USSR) in 1922. Under the aegis of the USSR, in December of that year, Georgia, Armenia, and Azerbaijan were once again united, this time as the Transcaucasian Federated Soviet Socialist Republic. Soviet authority remained weak in the region, however, as local branches of the Communist Party were very small and not well organized. To strengthen their control, Soviet leaders sent many Russians to the region to assume leadership roles. Most of these new leaders knew little about the Transcaucasus, resulting in policies that failed to take into account local needs and cultural norms.

One such policy was the collectivization of agriculture. For centuries, farming in the Transcaucasus had been carried out on small, family-owned plots as well as larger properties that were parceled out to tenant farmers. This system had created a tradition of private land ownership as well as a competitive and efficient market. Collectivization, on the other hand, forced independent and tenant farmers off their land and into large, state-owned enterprises. The immediate effect in the Transcaucasus was inefficiency and food shortages, as the new officials in charge of the collective farms were not familiar with local markets and distribution systems.

Soviet authorities now dictated what farms in the region would grow, and their decisions often failed to take into account local needs and strengths. For example, in fertile western Georgia, for centuries the country's rich breadbasket, farmers had to abandon wheat and other cereal grains and, according to the Soviet plan, specialize in tea and citrus fruit. The shift to new crops took time, and shortages in essential foodstuffs soon developed. The Soviet planners replaced locally grown wheat and cereal with imports from other parts of the USSR, forcing Georgia into an ever greater dependence on the central government in Moscow.

When the leaders the Soviets installed encountered widespread resistance to these drastic changes, they responded with force. To suppress dissent and to break the people's loyalty to their old leadership, the Soviets arrested those individuals who had held positions in the previous independent governments or who were considered nationalists. Houses of worship—potential centers of political opposition—were closed and their land and buildings seized. Anyone speaking out against these actions joined their former leaders in jail.

To ensure continued loyalty to the government in Moscow, the Soviet leaders also saw to it that young Armenians, Georgians, and Azerbaijanis were educated in the new Soviet schools. Here teachers indoctrinated students in the history of the Bolshevik Revolution and in the economic theories of Karl Marx, the founder of communism, and of Lenin, the Bolshevik

Soviet policy forced independent farmers to work on state-run collective farms.

GENOCIDE IN ARMENIA

Armenians living under Turkish rule were the first victims of the World War I–era confrontation between Armenia and Turkey. Beginning in 1915, the Turkish government planned and carried out a brutal genocide of the Armenian population of eastern Turkey. The first of its kind in modern times, the Armenian genocide resulted in large-scale massacres, forced deportations into the deserts to the south, and the deaths of more than 1.5 million Armenians. By the end of the genocide, which was obscured by the lack of communications and the distraction of the world war in western Europe, there were virtually no Armenians left in the eastern Turkish provinces. Armenian refugees streamed into neighboring Syria, into Russian Armenia, and into immigrant Armenian communities throughout the world. The Turkish government still denies a part in the genocide, but memory of the incident remains an obstacle to peace and stability in the Transcaucasus region.

revolutionary. To get a good education, or to hope for a rewarding career, one had to study or work under the control of the Communist Party, which also guided its members into positions far from their homes. While ensuring loyal and compliant leaders, this practice weakened local communities when their most promising young people left the region.

ANOTHER WORLD WAR

While the Soviet Union undertook a crash campaign of industrialization in the 1930s, Germany rebounded from its defeat in World War I under the leadership of dictator Adolf Hitler and the Nazi Party. Germany invaded Poland in 1939, touching off World War II. In the summer of 1941, German armies invaded western Russia and drove through the plains to the north of the Black Sea.

Unlike the earlier world conflict, World War II left the Transcaucasus relatively unscathed. Hitler's ultimate goal in southern Russia was to capture the oil fields of Azerbaijan near Baku and the Caspian Sea. Although the Germans reached the Volga River, which feeds the Caspian from the north, they were stopped at the great wall of the Caucasus. Only scattered ground fighting took place in this region, which remained in the hands of the Red Army. The German armies were eventually thrown back, and Germany surrendered in the spring of 1945.

The war had ravaged western Russia, but the Transcaucasus escaped with little damage. By the 1950s, the region had been completely transformed. Once a largely agricultural region, the region now played its assigned role in making the Soviet Union an industrial and military superpower. In the process, however, the Transcaucasus had lost its economic self-sufficiency. Goods and services that had once been produced in the Transcaucasus now were only available from distant sources throughout the Soviet Union.

Industrialization did bring improved roads, railways, and communication systems, particularly in Armenia. As a noted author recognizes, the Armenian economy "experienced high rates of growth in the agricultural and industrial sectors. Armenia has some heavy industry, the major examples being the controversial aluminum and chemical complexes in Yerevan." [12] But the changes also carried huge costs, which included environmental damage, since Soviet priorities in developing the Armenian economy included little or no regard for the environment or for public health.

The Transcaucasus was virtually unaffected by the German invasion of the Soviet Union during World War II.

The economic and political stability imposed on the Transcaucasus proved only temporary. By the late 1970s and early 1980s, the Soviet economy was rapidly declining, in large measure due to the USSR's ruinously expensive arms race with the United States. As more resources and workers were shifted from production of consumer to military goods and to heavy industry, Soviet economic problems worsened. The shoddy goods produced by Soviet factories found no market abroad; without an active foreign trade, the country could not afford to import consumer goods. Throughout the Soviet Union, the central planning system brought inefficiency, stagnant wages, and shortages of housing, automobiles, appliances, and furniture. While the rival capitalist nations of the West enjoyed economic growth, and their workers a steadily rising standard of living, the worsening economic situation within the Soviet Union meant that another revolution was almost inevitable.

The expensive arms race with the United States led to the rapid decline of the Soviet economy.

THE FALL OF THE SOVIET EMPIRE

Instead of providing logic and order to the production and marketing of goods, the Soviet Union's system of central plan-

ning was causing inefficiency and incredible waste. In cities throughout the Transcaucasus, many essential goods were growing scarce on market shelves. To buy food, housewives often had to wait in the long lines that formed whenever a shop was delivered its consignment of goods from distant warehouses. To buy an automobile or a television set, families had to place their names on waiting lists and wait—sometimes for months or years.

Similar problems plagued the delivery of important services. The vaunted Soviet health system was stymied by a shortage of physicians and a lack of medicines. Apartments were hard to come by, and those who finally obtained one usually had to share their living quarters with other families in cramped, unhealthy, and very stressful conditions.

Mikhail Gorbachev's programs of perestroika and glasnost led to the eventual collapse of the Soviet Union.

As the economic decline of the Soviet Union worsened through the mid-1980s, Soviet leader Mikhail Gorbachev, who came to power in 1985, attempted a radical reform of the Soviet system. He identified these changes with two key Russian words. Perestroika (Russian for "restructuring," specifically, economic restructuring) would provide incentives for workers to produce more goods of better quality. Glasnost, or openness, was meant to bring some accountability to the Soviet economic system. This policy ended the practice of covering up waste, inefficiency, and corruption on the part of factory managers as well as government officials. By holding accountable those who made mistakes, or who committed fraud, Gorbachev hoped to ease the widespread shortages and encourage people throughout the Soviet Union to work harder. In some cases, those found guilty of corruption were severely punished. Some were even executed.

For the nations of the Transcaucasus the reforms of perestroika were a welcome change from the traditional Soviet practices. Whereas decisions on what and how much to produce had once been made in faraway Moscow, under perestroika Armenians, Georgians, and Azerbaijanis gained greater control over their local economies. They could base their decisions on local needs and abilities, thereby promoting greater efficiency and, it was hoped, long-overdue economic growth. Perestroika also forced each republic to develop economic sectors that had languished for decades. Although Gorbachev believed his policy would help economic growth in the long run, the immediate result in the Transcaucasus and elsewhere was further hardship. A shortage of fertilizer and tools occurred in Georgia, while fuel shortages hindered Armenian industry. In Azerbaijan, the rapid pace of reform did not account for the supply of labor and materials in that the expansion of energy production required more skilled workers than the small republic had available.

At the same time that perestroika was causing hardship for many, glasnost was giving the people of the Transcaucasus a long-sought, independent political voice. Whereas the Soviet government had once strictly controlled all information and media distribution via radio, television, and newspapers, the new policy allowed writers and broadcasters some limited independence. While the Communist Party had been the only legal political party since the 1920s, glasnost allowed the formation of new political parties whose leaders did not necessarily follow the official line handed down by the leaders and bureaucrats in Moscow.

In the Transcaucasus, the effect of glasnost went beyond Gorbachev's stated intention of reforming and strengthening Communist rule and the Soviet state. In fact, the Soviet leader's reforms had quite the opposite effect. A few non-Communists were elected to the Georgian parliament, which, by 1991, had adopted the traditional Georgian flag (which had been replaced in the 1920s by the Soviet symbol of the hammer and sickle). In the spring of 1991, the people of Georgia elected a fervent anti-Communist, Zviad Gamsakhurdia, as their new president. In Azerbaijan, the Popular Front emerged to demand outright independence. Meanwhile, the people of Armenia had replaced the monolithic Communist Party leadership with a legislative body that included non-Communists.

Events soon proved that Gorbachev had miscalculated. In 1990 the Armenian leaders demanded total independence from Moscow. Gorbachev intended to reform the Soviet Union, not break it apart, so the request was denied. The leaders in Moscow still looked on the fifteen member republics as Soviet possessions, and their country as an unbreakable union of

THE COMMONWEALTH OF INDEPENDENT STATES

In an attempt to pull together the remnants of the Soviet empire, a group of former republics established the Commonwealth of Independent States (CIS) after the collapse of the Soviet Union. Armenia joined the commonwealth in December 1991, and Azerbaijan followed soon thereafter. Although it had the closest ties to the Slavic states to the north, Georgia did not join the CIS until October of 1993.

The Commonwealth of Independent States turned out to be a failure. Without a constitution in effect or a military to enforce and protect borders, and with wildly varying needs and problems, the states that made up the CIS had nothing to bind them together. By the mid-1990s, the Commonwealth of Independent States was merely a title without substance, a largely forgotten alliance whose members no longer work together economically, politically, or militarily.

Representatives from the CIS nations address religious and political issues during a press conference in December 2000.

states united in a common cause. And despite Gorbachev's ambitious intentions, perestroika did not solve the Soviet Union's economic problems. It became clear that the Soviet economic system was beyond repair while the inefficiencies of central planning remained in place. The people of the Transcaucasus approved of their new political freedoms, as well as the public accountability of glasnost. Yet they demanded more.

NATIONALISM ERUPTS

The political effects of glasnost also had the effect of bringing to the fore long-standing internal disputes among the people of the Transcaucasus. While proclaiming their allegiance to Gorbachev and his policies, the Armenians, for example, demanded annexation of the region of Azerbaijan known as Nagorno-Karabakh, where a majority of the population was Armenian. In parts of Georgia, Abkhazians and Ossetians demanded greater political autonomy from the Georgian government. Their demands, however, were opposed by ethnic Georgians living in these same areas, who wanted to remain under the authority of a Georgian government. In Azerbaijan, ethnic Armenians fought with Azerbaijanis in the city of Sumgait.

With little warning, the policies that Gorbachev had unleashed brought chaos to the Soviet Union as one republic after another began to seek self-rule. After a failed coup against Gorbachev in the summer of 1991, the Baltic states asserted their independence, as did Ukraine and the republics of central Asia. People long held under the domination of Moscow came out into the streets to parade and demonstrate in favor of independence, and there was very little the Soviet government or the Soviet army could do to prevent it.

Agitation for greater autonomy escalated to demands for outright freedom for the Transcaucasus. Armenians renewed their efforts toward independence, and in a referendum held in September 1991, they voted for independence, setting an example soon followed by the people of Georgia. A few months later, Azerbaijanis voted for independence through a national referendum.

The Union of Soviet Socialist Republics formally dissolved itself in December 1991. The previously captive states of the Transcaucasus, like all the former Soviet republics, were left to fend for themselves. Although they had finally achieved a long-sought goal, the three newly independent republics of the Transcaucasus were still caught unprepared. As a former U.S. military expert writes:

> The dissolution of the Soviet Union, therefore, came as a surprise . . . at a time when none of [the republics were] well prepared for it. Moreover, the massive bureaucratic institutions of the Soviet political systems were designed to insure a highly centralized state. The new de jure inde-

pendence, therefore, coexisted with the old de facto sub-ordination to Soviet Institutions. [13]

To prevent a complete breakdown of authority and public order, and to develop the needed free-market economies, the Transcaucasus republics had to quickly build new national institutions to replace the fallen Soviet bureaucracy.

NEW REPUBLICS

In Georgia, the transformation to independence was accompanied by violent political turmoil. President Gamsakhurdia ordered a crackdown on his opponents that was, in many ways, just as severe as any that had occurred under Communist officials and the Soviet state police. At the same time, ethnic groups demonstrating for self-rule fought pitched battles with police and the Georgian national guard in the streets of Tbilisi and other Georgian towns.

A group of Armenian nationalists protests against various anti-Armenian programs in Azerbaijan.

SHARED CHALLENGES

Each of the now-independent Transcaucasian republics faced a different challenge. In a French historian's assessment:

> Each of the three republics, of course, charted its own course and road to independence by relying on cultural heritage (different in each case) and natural resource endowment (similarly unique). But history and geography also provide reasons for viewing prospective sovereignty in the context of shared attributes, i.e., with each republic representing integral parts of a broader Transcaucasian region. [14]

The Transcaucasian republics had three important attributes in common. Most important was a common faith in the virtues of independence and self-sufficiency. None of the Transcaucasian republics desired to return to its old status as the colony of a more powerful nation, even for the sake of economic development or self-defense. Armenians, Georgians and Azerbaijanis all believed that independence was a positive development that would allow each of them to fully realize their potential. Having overcome the constraints of living in the Soviet Union, the three nations could act in their own national interest, making important decisions for their own people.

A second factor working for the Transcaucasus was its geography. Armenia could expand trade links with neighboring Iran, with its ally Russia, and even with its old nemesis, Turkey. Azerbaijan would serve as a cultural and economic bridge between Turkey and the culturally related states of central Asia that lie east of the Caspian Sea. Georgia's ports along the Black Sea would provide key outlets for industry and agriculture in landlocked Armenia and Azerbaijan.

The third shared attribute, the natural resources of the Transcaucasus, promised self-sufficiency, even prosperity. The subtropical climate allowed local growers to market citrus fruits, tea, tobacco, cotton, and silk. Oil and natural gas would always find buyers in a world in need of fuel, as would the hydroelectric power generated by Transcaucasian rivers. Under Soviet control, the Transcaucasus had also developed specialized industries, such as chemical production and the manufacturing of agricultural tools. Tourism and foreign trade promised to bring in foreign currency, essential for new investment in manufacturing and energy.

ROOTS OF ETHNIC CONFLICT

The reality of independence did not match these early expectations, however, largely due to the emergence of ethnic conflict, which brought a breakdown in trade, damaging blockades and boycotts, and the emigration of skilled and educated workers. Much of the ethnic conflict emerged hand-in-hand with the nationalism spurred by the collapse of the Soviet Union. As journalist Elizabeth Fuller writes, "The most overt manifestations of nationalism in the Transcaucasus have taken the form of interethnic conflict." [15] The people of the Transcaucasus have suffered from xenophobia, racism, political extremism, and even early signs of genocidal "ethnic cleansing."

Considering the history of the Transcaucasus, the eruption of ethnic conflict was predictable. As an observer notes, "Ethnically and culturally, the Caucasus [was] the most heterogeneous region of the Soviet Union. It [was] not only linguistically and religiously complex, but the various peoples of the Caucasus differed enormously in the extent to which they had formed a modern national consciousness when they were incorporated into the Soviet system." [16]

Violence among various ethnic groups became common once the Soviet Union withdrew from the Transcaucasus.

The clash of different cultures and traditions resulted in nationalistic rivalry. Armenians and Georgians both founded nations on the Western model. They both had a national religion, a national literary tradition, and an identity as independent states for centuries before the Russians arrived. The Azerbaijanis, on the other hand, prided themselves on their Turkic identity and Persian-Islamic heritage, and have constructed national symbols related to this history. Soon after the sudden, and rather peaceful, end of the Soviet Union, this rivalry triggered a period of violence and hardship in the Transcaucasus that bloomed into outright warfare in the Armenian enclave of Nagorno-Karabakh.

THE LEGACY OF SOVIET RULE

Ethnic and national conflicts were not the only problems that people of the Transcaucasus had to face. Education and health care that had once been subsidized by Moscow now had to be paid for out of the pockets of workers and their families. Industries organized and directed by Soviet planners had to survive as profitable concerns, competing with each other and with foreign businesses operating in the international marketplace. Energy, derived from oil, coal, hydropower, and thermal plants, had to be either produced or imported. An independent military had to be established. The people of the Transcaucasus would have to rebuild roads and railways. Under Soviet rule, and especially in the chaotic economy of the 1980s, resources had been scarce and essential infrastructure such as bridges, roads, railroads, and utilities had been neglected.

The seven decades of Soviet rule in the Transcaucasus also left behind a long trail of environmental damage, especially along the shores of the Caspian Sea. Home to the sturgeon that produced most of the Soviet Union's valuable caviar, the Caspian has been damaged by years of industrial development, a lack of environmental safeguards, and oil and natural gas drilling and exploration in various offshore fields.

The landscape of Armenia has also undergone brutal treatment. As occurred elsewhere in the Transcaucasus, seven decades of Soviet rule brought an unhealthy accumulation of industrial waste from toxic dumping. Soviet-era strip mining and timber cutting have also done serious environmental damage. Hydroelectric projects on rivers feeding into Lake Sevan have drained some 40 percent of the lake's increasingly polluted water.

THE RISE OF THE CASPIAN

Azerbaijan now must worry about a rise in the level of this salty inland sea. In the past fifteen years, the Caspian Sea has risen almost seven feet, occasionally flooding nearby villages, factories, and farmland. The sea has reclaimed some 12,300 square miles of land around it. As it spreads, it remains shallow (at a distance of nineteen miles offshore, the depth in some places reaches a mere five feet).

The damage to residents and buildings around the Caspian is not limited to Azerbaijan. In Russia, the rising Caspian is now threatening some one hundred villages and small towns and has damaged over six hundred miles of power lines. In Iran, the waters have advanced by over ten miles. Flooding in the town of Cheleken, which lies within Turkmenistan on the eastern shore of the Caspian, has ruined houses and a large chemical factory. Kazakhstan has lost more than twelve square miles of territory, and entire villages now lie underwater.

The rising Caspian also threatens the economies of the region. After decades of industrial polluting and the dumping of toxic waste into its waters, the Caspian has become an environmental disaster area. The poisoned waters threaten to engulf valuable wetlands and bring ecological devastation to the stocks of fish, including the prized sturgeon. For many Azerbaijanis, the Caspian Sea's large offshore deposits of oil and natural gas represent their nation's most valuable economic asset. But the rising Caspian has also become the country's biggest environmental challenge.

Decades of pollution have turned the Caspian Sea into an environmental disaster area.

The people of the Transcaucasus have demanded that their governments admit the severity of environmental problems and take steps to repair the damage. Many have called for regulation of polluting industries, especially the chemical industry, and the closure of nuclear power plants. But the repair of the environmental damage costs money, and it can also hinder industrial and energy production that is vital to economic recovery. Troubled by economic decline and stubborn ethnic conflict, and surviving with the weak support of volatile and hard-pressed electorates, the political leaders of the region often place environmental concerns well down on their list of priorities.

THE HARD ROAD TO INDEPENDENCE

The Transcaucasus nations emerged from the fall of the Soviet Union facing economic, political, and social problems. The legacy of economic decline and political instability also made it difficult to calm the ethnic violence of the region. Worse, the three republics could not find common cause nor common solutions to these conflicts. As researcher Elizabeth Fuller explains, "Because of their diverse geopolitical, economic and social conditions— and their diverse histories— the challenges faced by each have been unique in range and character."[17]

TROUBLE IN NAGORNO-KARABAKH

The oldest and most violent of these ethnic disputes has been the conflict over Nagorno-Karabakh, an enclave with an Armenian majority that lies entirely within Azerbaijan. The complicated issues surrounding Nagorno-Karabakh resemble no other conflict in the Transcaucasus.

The conflict goes back many years. Control over the region was transferred to Azerbaijan from Armenia when the Soviet leader Joseph Stalin imposed Soviet rule over the Transcaucasus in 1924. At that time, the native Armenians in Karabakh comprised more than 94 percent of the total population of 132,000. This Armenian majority steadily decreased to only 76 percent of the population between 1923 and 1979, after years of anti-Armenian discrimination by the Azeri government. Despite their shrinking majority, as the Soviet Union weakened, the Armenians living in Nagorno-Karabakh attempted to return the region to Armenian control. In a referendum held in December 1991, the Karabakh Armenians voted to leave the Soviet Union and unite

Joseph Stalin imposed Soviet rule over the Transcaucasus in 1924.

with Armenia, which had already declared its own independence from the Soviet Union.

Azerbaijan, however, was not about to allow the loss of this large territory. The fighting that followed, which killed more than twenty-five thousand and forced more than half a million refugees out of the region, resolved nothing. Nagorno-Karabakh failed to win recognition, either by Azerbaijan or by the rest of the world. Although the Armenians of Nagorno-Karabakh rely on the government of Armenia to represent their concerns in peace talks that have been underway for the past decade, the conflict has not been settled.

ARMENIA UNDER BLOCKADE

The dispute over Nagorno-Karabakh poisoned the already uneasy relations between Azerbaijan and Armenia. Azeri leaders accused Armenia of trying to annex Nagorno-Karabakh and, in response to this perceived threat, sealed Armenia's eastern border and shut down a natural gas pipeline that traverses the two countries. The blockade led to a faltering economy, food shortages, and nearly impossible living conditions within Armenia. Starved for fuel and electricity, more than two-thirds of Armenian industry ground to a complete halt.

Armenia's government responded by reversing its opposition to nuclear power and, in December 1992, reopening the country's only nuclear power plant, closed since the fall of 1988. Outside Armenia, this aging reactor is considered to be one of the most dangerous in the world. Yet it produces enough electricity to fulfill nearly half of Armenia's electricity demand and export power to Georgia as well.

Reopening one old nuclear power plant could not solve Armenia's problems, however. One observer explains that Armenia, during the winter of 1992–1993, "was on the brink of collapse. With sub-zero temperatures, industry at a standstill, fuel almost nonexistent . . . the population remained indoors huddled around makeshift stoves fueled by anything wooden, including door frames and furniture. The atmosphere was one of the utmost severity and depression." [18] The severe energy crisis led the residents to cut down trees from public gardens and squares for firewood. Anecdotes and stories painted a picture of gloom and despair:

> Residents of my building discovered one day this summer
> that the huge wooden outside door to the building was

ARMENIAN EMIGRATION

One of the most serious threats to Armenia's future is emigration. Throughout the 1990s, thousands of Armenians took advantage of their newfound freedoms to escape ethnic conflict and the country's dire economic situation. These economic and political refugees settled in Europe, the Middle East, Canada, and the United States. Armenian government statistics showed that between seventy-five thousand and eighty-five thousand Armenians left the country in 1999, about double the number who left in 1997 and 1998.

Many Armenians abroad provide their homeland with crucial foreign exchange, in the form of remittances (money sent back to their families). Some also return to invest in new businesses. But the migration is undermining the government's attempts at economic reform, because most of those who leave are skilled and educated citizens. As members of Armenia's upper socioeconomic class, they are the ones best able to get the country back on its feet. But the common feeling in Armenia has been that those who can afford to will leave, and those who cannot afford to leave must stay.

missing. It turned out that a first-floor neighbor had taken the door off its hinges and hidden it in the basement, hoping to use it as firewood this winter. The rest of us regretted that we did not think of it first. [19]

NEW LEADERS IN AZERBAIJAN AND ARMENIA

The leaders of Armenia were hard-pressed to find a solution to the country's many problems. In 1991 Levon Ter Petrosian, a linguist and a leading member of the Armenian nationalist movement, had become the first person elected president of an independent Armenia in more than seventy years. Ter Petrosian enjoyed widespread popularity at the beginning of his term, but several of his actions—a ban on opposition parties and censorship of the press—were criticized as undemocratic abuses of power. Support for Ter Petrosian began to seriously decline as his close advisers and family members were caught up in corruption scandals and illegal activities, including several politically motivated murders. He also lost popularity after attempting to compromise with Azerbaijan over Nagorno-Karabakh. After being reelected in a presidential election

President Levon Ter Petrosian (right) of Armenia met with President Ayaz Mutalibov (left) of Azerbaijan in an attempt to settle the dispute over Nagorno-Karabakh.

marred by accusations of vote rigging and voter intimidation, Ter Petrosian was forced to resign.

Azerbaijan had to deal with internal turmoil as well, as Communists who had prospered under Soviet rule battled nationalists who wanted to sever all ties with the past. During the early 1990s, the Communists, under President Ayaz Mutalibov, struggled to retain power. Both sides took their fight to the embattled enclave of Nagorno-Karabakh, where ethnic Armenians died by the thousands in the crossfire between the Azeri military and the anti-Communist Popular Front. Violent demonstrations in Baku and elsewhere forced Mutalibov to resign his post in the early spring of 1992.

In June 1992, the leader of the nationalist Azerbaijani Popular Front, Abulfez Elchibey, was elected to a five-year term. Before he ran for office, Elchibey had been a college professor but had also been involved in politics—at considerable personal risk. In 1975 the KGB, the Soviet secret police, arrested Elchibey, who was sentenced to a two-year jail term for actions "against the state." Although he won the 1992 election by a sizable margin, Elchibey and his party quickly began to lose their appeal. The setbacks in Nagorno-Karabakh, a worsening economy, political stalemate, and government corruption again drove the people of Azerbaijan to exasperation, and Elchibey was forced out of office in June 1993. Elchibey lived in virtual exile in his native Naxçivan until his death from cancer in a Turkish military hospital in August 2000.

Elected president of Azerbaijan in 1992, Abulfez Elchibey was forced out of office one year later.

GAMBLING IN ARMENIA

As the economic situation in Armenia worsens, some are exploiting the desperation by opening casinos and other gambling establishments. In the capital of Yerevan, and in the freezing months of winter, a common sight is long lines of people waiting outside the many gambling dens that operate in the city.

The dire economic conditions have led a large proportion of Armenians into gambling, which was not previously a particularly popular pastime. Many people say that gambling is their only hope for economic gain, a hope that does not rest on the promises of politicians or economists. Two leading gambling firms, "Family Lotto" and "Kind Lotto," report weekly lottery ticket sales of three hundred thousand—a disturbingly high number in a country with slightly more than 3 million residents. Perhaps most disturbing is the fact that gambling fever has made luck a greater virtue than the Armenians' traditional reliance on hard work.

ECONOMIC TURMOIL

Azerbaijan was fighting another battle to stabilize a weakened economy. The Soviet so-called Five-Year Plans had emphasized the development of energy production in Azerbaijan, at the expense of that republic's agriculture. Energy imports earned the Soviet treasury much-needed hard currency, and so the limited money was diverted from Azerbaijan's farms and from necessary maintenance of roads and other infrastructure. Tractors, combines, and other essential farm equipment went unrepaired and poorly maintained. Highways that linked rural areas to the cities went years without repair or modernization, making it impossible at times for Azeri farms to deliver their harvests to local markets.

Throughout the Transcaucasus, each nation found itself hamstrung by the old Soviet model of economic specialization, in which certain industries benefited from new government investment and others were completely neglected. One analyst claims that the economic obstacles in the Transcaucasus "cast serious doubt on their ability to survive as independent sovereign states."[20] Armenia, for example, has highly developed chemical and electronics industries. However, the nation lacks the energy sources these industries need and, because of the Azeri blockade, must rely on energy imports from Russia that must transit neighboring Georgia.

In Georgia, where the people were used to one of the highest standards of living in the Soviet Union, unemployment and energy shortages had been relatively unknown. But decisions made in Moscow eventually had damaging effects. In accordance with Soviet planning, most investment went to the industries of the cities, causing dire problems on Georgia's state-owned and collective farms. As a result, rural people flocked to the cities in search of jobs, a migration that caused housing shortages and put great strains on medical and social services.

ABKHAZIA

Georgia also had ethnic conflicts to deal with. The Abkhazians of northwestern Georgia clamored for total independence, and the people of South Ossetia sought to unite with their ethnic kin across the border in Russia. Paramilitary groups that answered to various warlords fought pitched battles while the Georgian government, with no national army of its own, stood by helplessly.

In 1992, at Georgia's request, Russian troops were deployed into South Ossetia, an action that solved nothing. Fighting continued into 1996, when the South Ossetians held local elections, which Georgia' s government promptly declared invalid. By the end of 1996, Georgia and South Ossetia, however, had agreed to stop using force against each other, establishing a fragile truce.

The conflict over Abkhazia did not turn out quite so well. Abkhazian separatism brought about a major military clash in 1992–1993. With support from armed groups from the northern

Members of the Georgian militia battle with Abkhazian rebels over control of Sukhumi, the regional capital.

Caucasus, and helped by Russian military forces stationed in the region, the Abkhazians defeated the Georgian militias sent into the region and gained full control of their region of the country. The conflict forced several hundred thousand ethnic Georgians from their homes. This refugee flight turned the Abkhazians, once a minority of 17 percent, into a majority in the region.

The United Nations stepped into the conflict and in April 1994 managed to broker a peace agreement. Abkhazia and Georgia agreed to a cease-fire, and twenty-five hundred Russian troops were stationed in Abkhazia to keep the peace. Thousands of Georgian refugees began returning, while Abkhazia agreed to become an autonomous region within the Georgian republic. In November, however, Abkhazia adopted a new constitution and declared its complete independence.

After winning reelection in November 1995, President Eduard Shevardnadze of Georgia retaliated by asking a grouping of former Soviet republics, the Commonwealth of Independent States, for economic sanctions against Abkhazia—by Georgian law, still a part of his own country. The CIS agreed in January 1996, and the Georgian militia and the Abkhazians again picked up their weapons. Sporadic fighting continues into the twenty-first century, with Russian soldiers standing by ineffectively while Abkhazia and Georgia trade shots and shells across their border and refugees flee from burning homes and wrecked villages.

THE NEW BOSSES

After the fall of the Soviet Union, all three nations of the Transcaucasus adopted constitutions that provided for popularly elected leaders. But democracy was an unfamiliar tradition in the former Soviet republics, and seventy years of Soviet government left a legacy of dictatorship and despotism. Government institutions that were supposed to guarantee liberty for the people instead suppressed their constitutional freedoms, rendering the citizens impotent against those who sought to seize and hold power by force.

The people of the Transcaucasus found themselves turning to their old Soviet-era leaders for guidance in the troubled times after independence. When internal conflict overwhelmed Azerbaijan in the summer of 1993, the people elected Geidar Aliyev as their president in the fall of that year. Aliyev's face was familiar to them: He had been Azerbaijan's Commu-

nist Party boss in the era of glasnost and perestroika. It was now his turn to deal with a declining economy and the costly military conflict over Nagorno-Karabakh.

Born in 1923 in Naxçivan, the small enclave of Azeri territory that lies southwest of Armenia, Aliyev followed a career in the Soviet intelligence service, the KGB, reaching the position of chairman of the Azeri branch of the KGB in 1967. As a senior official of the Azerbaijani Communist leadership in 1969, he made a career of arresting Azeri nationalists throughout the 1970s. He strongly supported the Soviet invasion in Afghanistan in 1979 and was rewarded for his loyalty by an appointment to the Politburo, the committee of the top Soviet ministers, in 1982.

In 1987, however, Soviet leader Mikhail Gorbachev fired Aliyev from the Politburo. Aliyev returned to his hometown in Naxçivan and quietly waited for his next opportunity. In 1990 he was elected to the Naxçivan regional parliament as a nationalist. As the Communists gradually lost control of the Soviet Union, Aliyev declared that he was quitting the Communist Party. After the Soviet Union disintegrated in 1991, he called for total independence for Azerbaijan. Although he professed loyalty to Azerbaijan, he also advocated autonomy for his home region,

Geidar Aliyev (center) was elected president of Azerbaijan in the fall of 1993.

Naxçivan. As the new chairman of the regional parliament, for example, he signed treaties in 1991 with both Turkey and Iran without even checking first with the Azeri government in Baku.

In the meantime, the government of Abulfez Elchibey was in turmoil. In June 1993, Elchibey ordered troops to march on a defiant army garrison in the town of Ganca. The garrison, led by Colonel Surat Huseinov, turned the tables on Elchibey by marching on the capital and seizing control of the government. Elchibey fled to Naxçivan, and Aliyev returned to Baku, where the legislature voted to turn the presidency over to him.

In October 1993, Aliyev won Azerbaijan's presidential elections with almost 99 percent of the vote. Aliyev was soon involved in a bitter rivalry with Colonel Huseinov, whose troops staged mutinous uprisings in 1994 and 1995. Azerbaijan began sliding into civil war as forces loyal to Huseinov and Aliyev fought it out in the streets and highways. At one point, Aliyev declared a state of emergency, banned all public demonstrations, and banned rival political parties. In October 1998, he won a second five-year term with slightly more than 76 percent of the vote. Each of Aliyev's elections, however, has been tainted by evidence of voting irregularities and fraud.

EDUARD SHEVARDNADZE

Another prominent former Soviet official returned to Georgia in 1992. Eduard Shevardnadze, who had been the Soviet Union's foreign minister under Gorbachev, returned to his native Georgia, where President Zviad Gamsakhurdia had just been deposed and chased out of the capital of Tbilisi. Born in Georgia in 1928, Shevardnadze began his political career in the Georgian police and internal security forces, which he led as minister of internal affairs in 1965. In 1972 he became the Communist Party boss in Georgia. At this time, the people of the Soviet Union looked with cynicism and scorn at such career bureaucrats, whose good fortunes depended less on native skill or talent than on following the Party line and paying homage to those in higher positions. But by fighting corruption and encouraging economic growth in his republic, Shevardnadze was able to match the growing popularity of Georgian nationalists and was able to control early attempts by the Abkhazians to gain greater freedoms from Georgia.

NEW GOVERNMENTS IN THE TRANSCAUCASUS

Georgia
Georgia adopted its new constitution in August 1995. This constitution reinstated the office of the president, who was limited to two five-year terms. The president selects a cabinet of ministers, at the head of which sits a minister of state. The Georgian legislature of 235 members is elected every four years. Although twenty different parties contested the elections of 1999, only two parties, the Citizens' Union of Georgia and the All-Georgia Revival Union, won enough votes to place members in the legislature. The leading party, the Citizens' Union of Georgia, is also the party of President Eduard Shevardnadze, who won election to a second term in April 2000.

Georgia has three self-proclaimed autonomous regions: Abkhazia, Ajaria, and South Ossetia. Each of these states has its own body of elected legislators, but the Georgian government only recognizes Ajaria, which is the only one of the three that is not demanding independence.

Azerbaijan
The people of Azerbaijan voted for a new constitution in 1995. This document sets the term of the president at five years. The president appoints a prime minister and a council of ministers. The National Assembly is known among the Azeris as the *milli majlis*. The 125 members of this body are elected to five-year terms.

Azerbaijan officially divides itself into fifty-nine districts, eleven cities, and the republic of Naxçivan, which adheres to the new Azeri constitution. The only region of the country with no representation is Nagorno-Karabakh, which declared itself independent in December 1991. The Azeri government has refused to recognize Nagorno-Karabakh as independent, nor does it allow representatives of the region to sit in the assembly.

Armenia
Armenians voted for a new constitution in July 1995. As in the other Transcaucasian republics, the constitution established the office of president, who is elected to a term of five years. A prime minister heads a council of ministers and recommends their appointment to the president. The National Assembly of Armenia has 131 members, who serve four-year terms. The Pan-Armenian National Movement has the largest bloc of representatives in the assembly.

Armenia comprises ten regions, known as *marz*, which are led by governors appointed by the National Assembly. Local communities (*hamaynk*) elect their own leaders every three years.

Having risen to the important position of foreign minister under Gorbachev in 1985, Shevardnadze's reputation remained high among his countrymen in Georgia. He traveled widely outside the country, pitching Gorbachev's reforms and meeting with the most powerful leaders of Europe and North America. But by 1990, Shevardnadze was seeing that

*The former Soviet
foreign minister,
Eduard Shevardnadze
was elected president of
Georgia in 1995.*

the openness encouraged by Gorbachev was allowing nationalist movements in Georgia and elsewhere to get out of hand. Shevardnadze realized that the fall of Communist regimes in central Europe meant that the Soviet Union's own demise was fast approaching.

Shevardnadze resigned as Soviet foreign minister in 1990, although he returned for a brief time to the post in late 1991. He returned to his native Georgia, where he was elected to the parliament in 1992. His rise to the top spot was rapid. Shevardnadze became a member of the five-person ruling State Council in 1992 and then became chairman of the parliament later that year. He went on to become president in November 1995 and then won reelection to another five-year term as president in April 2000.

Despite his success at the polls, his past as Communist Party boss still lessens the appeal of Shevardnadze among many ordinary Georgian citizens. Many see a complete break with the past as Georgia's only hope to regain its balance. As Mikho Naneishvili, the leader of Georgia's Liberal Democratic Party, puts it:

> Those people [former Communist leaders] are no great lovers of capitalism. They may wish to think progressively, but they simply aren't trained to. The best we can say for them is that they are utterly devoted to Shevardnadze himself. Shevardnadze may wish to use his immense influence for the nation's benefit, but our other prominent politicians are more interested in power than principle. The ministries are full of unworthy people who have no expertise and can't be relied upon.[21]

WORKING TOGETHER

The economic, geographical, and political realities in the Transcaucasus provide motivation for the three nations to work together, and to a limited extent this has begun to happen. Armenia, for example, has gone to some trouble to foster strong relations with Georgia, in large part because Azerbaijan continues its strangling economic blockade. With some encouragement by Georgia, Armenia has also attempted to resolve its differences with Azerbaijan, although formal talks have not yet yielded improved relations.

The Georgian government, in turn, improved its own relationship with Azerbaijan during the 1990s, and both countries now benefit from economic cooperation. The Azerbaijani government

President Clinton participates in the signing of the cooperation treaty between Georgia and Azerbaijan in November 1999.

DAILY LIFE IN THE PRISONS

One little-known fact of life in the Transcaucasus has been terrible prison conditions. The living conditions of the region's prison facilities, already bad under the Soviet system, have worsened since independence. There has been no funding for even routine maintenance, and food shortages, a lack of heat and electricity, and unsanitary conditions have become the norm.

The importance of penal conditions goes beyond issues of crime and justice. In each of the three countries, there are many political prisoners, many of whom are arrested and jailed for belonging to opposition parties. The jailing of independent or opposition journalists is also not uncommon. Many political prisoners are held without charge and are not given the opportunity to defend themselves at trial.

There has been little attention given to prison conditions. But as disease and hunger are common occurrences, the governments must make the effort to improve prison conditions and end political imprisonment.

has promised Georgia a share of the profits from oil and natural gas production; in return, Georgia will allow Azerbaijan to build a pipeline through Georgian territory. The pipeline will allow Azerbaijan to transport its abundant oil and gas supplies to the markets of Western Europe through Georgia's Black Sea ports, while Georgian farmers and industry will benefit from a reliable source of energy.

Technically, the treaty that provides for economic cooperation between Azerbaijan and Georgia is also designed to isolate Armenia, since the agreement contains a promise by Georgia not to sell any of the oil or natural gas to Armenia. Georgia, however, has kept its border with Armenia open and has allowed a free flow of goods and energy from Russia to Armenia, which returns the favor by exporting electricity produced at its nuclear power plant to Georgia.

The problem of Nagorno-Karabakh remains a hot issue in the Transcaucasus and a source of constant tension between Armenia and Azerbaijan. The international community, through the United Nations and the Organization for Security and Cooperation in Europe (OSCE), has brought the leaders of the two countries to the negotiating table. These talks represent an important chance for ending the long years of conflict, if these leaders can overcome the deep mutual suspicion that has built up over the centuries.

5

Every Day Is a Struggle

The sudden fall of the Soviet Union left the Transcaucasus nations unprepared for a wrenching transition. The people faced a near-total loss of support from their governments. After years of relying on the old system's guarantees of work and social assistance, they suddenly had to struggle to obtain the basic necessities and to deal with shortages of food, inadequate housing, and the widespread loss of jobs.

As occurred elsewhere in the Soviet Union, the Transcaucasus republics went through a dramatic shift in population and demographics as industrialization took hold in the 1930s. The cities attracted increasing numbers of people in search of better-paying factory jobs and a better standard of living. As the population shifted from the rural villages and towns to the cities, the state built new and updated services, including roads, schools, hospitals, clinics, public transportation, and utility systems. Houses in the cities were equipped with telephones, running water, and central heat, amenities that were not commonly available in the villages. Stores and shops in the cities also had better selections of food and consumer goods. For the old people and the children living in the cities, there were more doctors and hospitals available; medicines were easier to find and cheaper than in the countryside.

As each country worked to develop a self-sufficient economy, workers faced lower wages and unemployment. Deprivation and competition for jobs in the city led some to miss the old Soviet system. Many pensioners and elderly in the Transcaucasus grew impatient with the promises of the new nationalist leaders. A common sentiment went something like this: As unjust and monolithic as the Soviet system was, it had at least guaranteed jobs, pensions, an education, and a minimum of free health care. The nationalists who replaced the Communists delivered very little, and seemed to guarantee only misery.

Nostalgia for the Communist past became so widespread in the Transcaucasus that politicians began to fear a Communist revival. In Armenia and Azerbaijan, many Soviet-era Communists returned to politics with the enthusiastic support of the people. Supporters of the nationalists argued that their countries had paid a high price under the Soviet system, and that independence and a multiparty democracy was the only hope for a brighter future.

EDUCATION, THE KEY TO A BETTER LIFE

Whether one works in a manufacturing plant in Armenia, on a farm in Georgia, or at an oil refinery in Azerbaijan, making ends meet has always been hard. For most people in the Transcaucasus, daily life is still a matter of just getting by. The key to a good career and a decent life under the Soviet system, and in the modern Transcaucasus, remains the same: a good education.

The Soviet system of free and mandatory education had resulted in nearly 100 percent literacy by the 1980s. In Georgia, the people enjoyed one of the highest rates of education in the Soviet Union. In 1989 more than 15 percent of adults had graduated from a university and more than 57 percent of the

Two Armenians sell gasoline to earn money. Because of high unemployment levels, citizens of the Transcaucasus must earn money by whatever means available.

population had completed secondary school. In Armenia, 14 percent of the adult population held university degrees, and 58 percent of Armenians over the age of fifteen had finished secondary school. Education in Azerbaijan was also expanded under the Soviet system, with 100 percent of Azerbaijani people between the ages of nine and fifty able to read and write.

But education has been hard hit by the economic problems of recent years. For youngsters, education is still valued, but advancement is limited by a lack of money to pay teachers and to maintain schools. Many schools in the region closed for good because of reductions in government spending and investment. Schools in Armenia have been disrupted by shortages of heating oil and fuel, and some are closed for months at a

CORRUPTION IN GEORGIA

Bribery, cheating, and a casual approach to written law long characterized the workings of the higher echelons of Soviet government and business. In the Transcaucasus, the situation was no different, and corruption among the people who share political and economic power still reigns. Georgia, in particular, suffers from a reputation of endemic corruption in business and politics. Michael Specter, in his article "Rainy Days in Georgia," which appeared in the *New Yorker* on December 18, 2000, carries this problem to the highest and most popular official in the land.

It is perhaps unfair to ask any single person to carry the weight of a nation, but for more than a decade [Eduard] Shevardnadze has been seen as the solution to all of Georgia's problems. Increasingly, however, and perhaps inevitably, many people also regard him as a principal cause. To achieve peace, he traded the idealism of his Gorbachev years for the pragmatism needed to bargain with warlords. If the warlords no longer run the country, a small group of wealthy and dishonest plutocrats do. Pensions average seven dollars a month and are infrequently paid. There is no real public sector. The government has made it easy for a few well-connected businessmen to snap up valuable state properties for almost nothing. Shevardnadze's son-in-law received a license to run one of Georgia's mobile-phone companies for fifteen dollars, far less than it would have cost him to buy a telephone.

time during the coldest months of the year. Schools and universities in all three countries are still faced with shortages of books, supplies, and adequate buildings. Many teachers have not been paid regular salaries for years, and in some cases have left their classrooms as a result. In September 2000, for example, teachers in an eastern part of Georgia refused to hold classes to protest the government's failure to pay them.

Since the fall of the Soviet Union, the quality and availability of medical care has significantly declined.

A SHARED PROBLEM: HEALTH CARE

Like education, medical care was a top priority for the Soviet Union, which often boasted of the free access to state hospitals and clinics enjoyed by its populace. Medical care for women and children was the most important priority in this system, although important government officials received preferential treatment. The Soviets did make dramatic improvements in medicine throughout the Soviet Union. All over the country, life expectancy rose while rates of disease fell. But the system did have its drawbacks. A shortage of prescription medicines affected all Soviet citizens, including those in the Transcaucasus, and medical care and supplies were lacking in rural areas. Because there were no nursing homes available for the care of the elderly, individual families had to take complete responsibility for the care of their aging relatives.

In Georgia, famous for the long lifespans of villagers, the average life expectancy now stands at sixty-nine for men and seventy-six for women. The country also enjoys a very low rate of cancer and ready access to medical personnel (almost sixty doctors for every ten thousand people in 1990). But in the aftermath of the breakup of the Soviet Union, the state has cut its financing to medical facilities, while worsening living conditions affect public health in many areas. Georgia has begun to suffer a shortage of hospital beds and a rising rate of infant mortality. This, coupled with a birth rate of just 9.1 per 1,000 population—the lowest in western Asia—means the nation has an annual population growth rate of just .15 percent.

There has been a similar decline in Armenia, where the population of 3.8 million makes this the smallest of all the Transcaucasus nations. Armenia has an annual growth rate of just .4 percent, but if emigration from Armenia continues at the rate it attained in the 1990s, the population may actually decrease. The large-scale emigration has turned many Armenian cities into virtual ghost towns. As one observer notes:

> Kapan, once a flourishing industrial center, is especially hard-hit: its population has dropped from 47,000 to 20,000 since independence. Its roads are lined with half-empty apartment blocks and abandoned factories. Its once noisy cafes are lifeless. In its open-air market, there are more sellers than buyers.... The main route out of Kapan is a mountainous road that is sprinkled with land mines. Still, people simply close the doors of their apartments, or sell them for as little as $600, and quietly board those buses. All over the country, people are desperate to get out any way they can.[22]

At one time, Armenia had the Soviet Union's lowest rates of cancer, tuberculosis, and infant mortality. After the fall of the Soviet Union, a trade blockade by neighboring Azerbaijan and Turkey caused an urgent shortage of medical supplies and made some medicines nearly impossible to obtain. In addition, energy shortages affected hospitals and clinics, whose staff and patients had to endure a lack of heat and electricity. In 1992 and 1993, healthy newborn babies and elderly patients were dying from the cold and a lack of medicine. By the end of 1993, more than half of the country's hospitals and clinics were closed due to shortages of electricity, heating fuel, and medical supplies.

Even under Soviet rule, the people of Azerbaijan had always suffered due to inadequate medical services. Hospitals and clinics were not provided with necessary equipment or supplies, and there were never enough beds for patients. The breakup of the Soviet Union only made the situation worse. In the 1990s, shortages of medicines, equipment, and qualified doctors continued, and a lack of sanitation worsened conditions in most hospitals and clinics. As in many of the former Soviet Republics, Azerbaijan is seeing a sharp fall in fertility rates, and infant mortality stands at 16.6 per 1,000 live births—the highest rate in the Transcaucasus.

ELECTION FRAUD IN AZERBAIJAN

The people of Azerbaijan were glad enough to throw off the shackles of Soviet power—but they could not always get rid of Soviet officials. As in many other countries of the Soviet bloc, former Communist Party officials simply changed their affiliations and their titles, and stayed right where they were. "What Next," an unsigned editorial in the *Economist* dated November 11, 2000, describes the well-merited cynicism of Azeri voters to the situation and to their erstwhile leader, Geidar Aliyev:

> Two elections took place in Azerbaijan on November 5th. In the official version, almost 70% of the electorate went to the polls, where people voted joyously and en masse for the ruling New Azerbaijan Party.

> . . . In reality, the poll was a damning indictment of the government. Independent observers reckoned that barely one-third of the electorate bothered to vote. And despite a barrage of favorable coverage on Azerbaijan's government-controlled television and the barring of hundreds of opposition candidates from the ballots, the governing party ran neck and neck with the main opposition, the Muslim Democratic Party, known as Musavat. Had the votes been fairly counted, Mr. Aliyev's lot would have failed by a long chalk to win a majority of seats.

> . . . The election was a farce. Panicky election officials struggled to top up the ruling party's votes. Foreign witnesses watched in astonishment as boxes were stuffed with false ballots and opposition politicians were threatened with arrest. Many observers were ejected from polling stations. Ambassador Gerard Stoudmann, head of the democracy and human-rights office within the Organization for Security and Co-Operation in Europe, called it "a crash course in the different methodologies of manipulation."

The medical problems and shortages continue, and health care throughout the Transcaucasus has reached a critical condition. Although aid from other nations has helped, the fundamental causes of these problems remain to be addressed. The impact of medical crises will also greatly hinder children's well-being and development in the Transcaucasus, adding yet another long-term problem to the economic and social woes that beset the region at the close of the twentieth century.

THE TATTERED SAFETY NET

The Soviet Union prided itself on a comprehensive safety net of social services, which extended to the workers and families of the Transcaucasus. For example, in 1985 nearly half of the Georgian state budget was spent on food and housing assistance and to finance health care and education. New mothers were granted a year and a half of partial maternity leave and all workers were guaranteed retirement pensions.

These programs abruptly ended with the fall of the Soviet Union. The new Transcaucasian governments were unable to pay for maternity leave, for food and housing assistance, or for pensions and unemployment benefits. The social safety net disappeared just as economic reforms were causing many people to lose their jobs. In Armenia, the situation is illustrated in the life of Sonya Toumanyan, a widow in her late sixties. Toumanyan lives alone, as her three living sons left Armenia to find better jobs in Russia. (A fourth son died in the fighting with Azerbaijan during the clashes of 1992.) Nearly all of her $6 monthly pension goes for electricity and some heat, and she manages to get discounted bread from a local bakery. For medicine, she turns to the few relief organizations that extend help to the elderly. She has asthma but receives enough medicine from the Armenian Relief Society to prevent attacks.

With the old social programs and benefits gone, the countries of the Transcaucasus have struggled to fill the gaps. Most measures, however, have not been well thought out or have been designed only to temporarily help ease the suffering. Longer-term programs simply lack the needed funding. For example, once Georgia became independent, its government changed its social welfare policies to make up for the loss of money from Moscow. A new social security fund, established in 1991, promised pensions for 1.3 million retired people as well as unemployment benefits and payments to single mothers and children. The fund represented an important assurance to the people of Georgia: They had someplace to turn to for help in times of need. Although the fund was financed by a national tax on workers, it has made only irregular and late payments to pensioners, due to the problems of collecting taxes. Many poorly paid workers who can barely provide for their own families resist making any further contributions to the state. Social welfare programs such as these are of little help for the average family. One Georgian complained to a visiting journalist that she was receiving a pension of about $6 a month, barely enough to buy a little bread.

Still, no matter how poorly planned or executed, such programs may be all that a family can count on. In Azerbaijan, for instance, several hundred thousand refugees live in temporary shelters and tents on the outskirts of the main cities. Those who have jobs may not fare all that well. The average monthly salary

With the social programs provided by the Soviet government gone, people in the Transcaucasus have struggled to make ends meet.

for an Azerbaijani worker is estimated at around $45 (as of October 2000), compared with the average $20 monthly pension.

In Armenia, only 35 percent of all workers received benefits from the government when they found themselves unemployed during an economic crisis that struck in 1993. This crisis occurred in a small country where many people had already been made homeless by a devastating earthquake that took place in 1988. By 1991 an astonishing eight hundred thousand people—24 percent of the population—were homeless. Two years later, 90 percent of the population were living below the official poverty line. As of September 2000, 42 percent of all Armenians (and about one-fifth of all Azerbaijani and Georgian workers) were earning less than $2 a day.

The dire situation is leading desperate people to new avenues for making ends meet, such as gambling. Armenian sociologist Aharon Adibekian writes that "the gambling boom results from the hopeless situation the people are now in. Gambling gives them hope for a better life, something that they have not gotten from government officials and politicians in the last ten years."[23]

THE ECONOMICS OF CHANGE

Economic reforms only added new pressures on already stressed governments. The Soviet Union's collapse stopped the flow of supplies and resources to nearly all factories and businesses in the region. The new governments struggled to maintain production to feed their people and to earn money to finance their budgets. They soon found themselves forced to sell many of the state-owned factories, which were operating inefficiently and at a loss. This privatization process was conducted through a series of sales—many of them rigged to benefit well-connected members of the new governments or their friends.

Privatization helped fund the public treasuries but left many workers without jobs, while a privileged elite benefited from buying state-owned companies cheaply. Profit, and not public welfare, drove these new owners, who cut jobs and slashed wages. Privatization also divided large, state-owned collective farms into smaller farms owned and operated by individuals and families. Private land ownership was an important agricultural reform, but one that came with a major drawback: The state could no longer provide essential fertilizer and seeds as it had in

the past. This brought a drop in production, which in turn worsened the already serious shortages of food. These shortages drove up prices for food, clothing, and other basic goods.

In Georgia, inflation was made more burdensome because wages and salaries failed to keep up with price increases. This was especially the case among state workers. Georgia's university professors, for example, were earning about $4 per month in 1993, while those working for the few Western companies active in the country were earning five to one hundred times as much. Wage inequalities such as this added to the problems of underfunded social programs, medical care, and education. Many people left their state jobs to make a better living in the private sector. It soon became common for professors and even medical staff to quit their jobs for work as taxi drivers, small businessmen, and peddlers.

In Armenia, the job losses due to privatization were compounded by factory closings and Azerbaijan's economic blockade. By the winter of 1993, the daily life of the Armenians reached its worst point. The average person at that time was earning only enough to pay for housing and transportation,

The privatization of state-owned factories has left many people unemployed in the Transcaucasus.

with a little left over from a month's pay to buy ten eggs or three hundred grams of butter. With so little money for food, malnutrition began to affect the population, especially the young and the elderly. By the mid-1990s, most Armenians who could afford to leave the country had done so.

In Azerbaijan, the difficult situation was helped slightly by the country's valuable oil supplies. Unlike Armenia and Georgia, which competed in the world economy with very little in the way of natural resources, Azerbaijan could sell oil to satisfy an insatiable world energy demand. Although transport of oil posed challenges, these sales have been an important source of income to the country. But the daily life of the ordinary person was not that much better than in Armenia and Georgia. In Azerbaijan in 1993, the government reported that the average income could pay only half of the most basic living expenses. It was also found that someone earning the minimum weekly wage could barely afford the price of one loaf of bread.

The struggles of daily life in the Transcaucasus can be met with new policies to provide social protection to the most vulnerable citizens. International aid agencies also have an important role to play. An improved standard of living is the key to regaining security and peace in the region. The economic stability of the ordinary family is the best way to end the conflict and misery that have prevailed during the past decade.

THE ART AND LITERATURE OF THE TRANSCAUCASUS

Each of the Transcaucasus countries boasts a long heritage of music, literature, and the arts. Influenced by history and by religious faith, each of these nations developed a distinct national style, which helped to preserve ethnic identity, even as the people were ruled by foreign empires. The constantly changing national boundaries that resulted from repeated conquests turned the Transcaucasus into a crazy-quilt mixture of languages, religions, literatures, and artistic styles. Students, performers, and artists bicker over what constitutes authentic traditional cultures. Meanwhile, some residents look to the future, and attempt to bring the Transcaucasus into the modern mainstream by developing new, international modes of communication, such as the World Wide Web and the Internet.

A CLASH OF ALPHABETS

One peculiarity of the Transcaucasus may remain a stubborn roadblock to international recognition and appreciation of the region's traditional cultures: the written alphabet, the basic building block of national culture. Each nation of the region has its own alphabet and each system has become a source of peaceful but sometimes bitter controversy over the very letters that are used for conveying information and expressing individual creativity.

Azerbaijan's situation is illustrative of how various cultural crosscurrents have resulted in a virtual maelstrom of linguistic problems. Written Azerbaijani traditionally used an Arabic script until the 1930s, but then the Soviet government forced a change to the Cyrillic alphabet that is commonly used in Russian and other Slavic languages. Although the now-independent Azerbaijan has adopted a Roman alphabet (that is, letters that look much like those in English), a controversy has arisen over whether the nation should return to using the old Arabic script, which would allow Azerbaijani readers to explore much important Islamic literature.

This link to Islamic texts is important, as Azerbaijan has been an Islamic nation since the seventh century. Nearly invisible behind the elaborate flourishes of this lettering are instructive passages from the Koran, the Islamic book of prayer. Moreover, Arabic script is more than simply a way of writing words: It is an art form in its own right. The traditional calligraphic arts associated with the Arabic language found their way into the Transcaucasus, where elaborate lettering appears on Azerbaijani pottery, metalwork, and sculpture.

A unique language has also played an important role in Armenian culture. The distinct, thirty-eight-letter Armenian alphabet bears no relation to Roman, Cyrillic, or Arabic lettering. (Interestingly, the closest relation to the Armenian alphabet is Ethiopian; the two systems share many nearly identical char-

Islam influences all aspects of language and culture in Azerbaijan.

acters. Armenian legend holds that the designer of the Armenian alphabet, a fifth-century monk named Mesrop Mashdotz, studied in an Ethiopian monastery, where he helped the Ethiopians create their native language. It seems just as plausible, however, that the Armenian monk was influenced by Ethiopian.)

Prior to the introduction of their alphabet, the Armenians had used Greek, Syriac, and Persian as the languages for their official documents. But the impetus for the alphabet was religious, not secular. The Armenian church developed a form of written Armenian, known to scholars as *grabar*, as a means of educating its followers in the Bible and in other religious works, which could be set down for the first time in the Armenian language.

The development of the Armenian alphabet allowed for new translations of books, poetry, and short stories previously inaccessible to speakers of Armenian. These medieval translations also exposed Armenian writers to the culture of Europe and other parts of the world. By the thirteenth century, the ancient *grabar* was gradually replaced by a modernized "Middle Armenian" writing style that reflected usages and idioms common elsewhere in Europe. While this modernization never affected the language used in the church, almost all of the secular literature of the period used the vernacular Middle Armenian language.

Experts place Armenian on a remote and separate branch of the Indo-European langage family. Some believe that Armenian developed from some extinct, non-Indo-European language, such as Aramaic, which was spoken in the ancient Middle East. Armenian has continued to evolve to the point that now everyday spoken Armenian has split into eastern and western dialects. The people of the Armenian republic and the Armenian communities in Iran use the eastern dialect, which was used in Russian- and Soviet-ruled Armenia. The western dialect was the language of Turkish-ruled portions of Armenia. The two dialects have somewhat different vocabularies and pronunciation, differing spellings of common names, and different grammar.

RELIGION AND CULTURE IN ARMENIA

Religious faith played a central role in Armenia, as in the other Transcaucasus republics, in the development of literature and the arts. In the fourth century A.D., Armenia became the first nation in the world to adopt the Christian church as its official religion. Ever since that time, Armenian artists and musicians have drawn on Christian themes and symbols for inspiration. Furthermore, the church often has been a source of training and support for Armenia's performing artists. Indeed, many of the best Armenian singers today began their careers in the choirs of churches and monasteries. The same can be said of aspiring singers in Georgia.

In Tbilisi and Yerevan, church art fairs provide an alternative to exhibitions in private galleries or in museums, many of which have gone out of business. Ordinary people attend religious events and celebrations amid collections of fine art. Painters in Georgia and Armenia seek out commissions for religious works, particularly the icons—paintings of Christ and the saints—that dominate the artwork of eastern (Orthodox) churches and homes. For artists, religious works provide a crucial source of income and churches are a convenient venue for displaying one's work.

A CLASH OF ALPHABETS

One of the crucial debates within Azerbaijan concerns the alphabet. In a quest to rid itself of the symbols of the Soviet past, such as the Cyrillic script used to write Russian, Azerbaijan officially adopted the Roman alphabet in December 1991. Yet old habits die hard, and while the Roman alphabet is used for all official documents such as passports and birth certificates, the Cyrillic alphabet still appears in notices, signs, and in every Azerbaijani newspaper, although the headlines are in Roman script. The fact that many newspapers have adopted Roman script for headlines has brought about a curious cultural phenomenon: Many younger Azerbaijanis can read only newspaper headlines, while their elders can read only the main text of newspaper articles.

The Azeri government has come up with laws requiring fluency in Azerbaijani for government officials, and requiring high school students to achieve passing grades in the study of Azerbaijani. Yet ten years after the official change, there is still work to be done. One crucial task still to be completed is the establishment of standard Roman fonts for use in computer programs and Internet communications. Until these letter designs can be settled, Azerbaijanis will be largely non-literate in high-tech industries and computer programming—a crippling handicap for a small nation trying to compete in a global market.

The Church of the Holy Cross (pictured) in Turkey is an example of Armenian architecture.

Architecture is another significant component of Armenian culture and has similarly been influenced by religion. Impressive temples, daunting military fortifications, and elaborate churches have survived from the fourth and fifth centuries. Religious architecture developed with the Armenian church, as native builders incorporated circular domes and other difficult techniques into their designs. A leading example of Armenian church architecture, the tenth-century Church of the Holy Cross, rises along the shores of Lake Van in modern Turkey.

As with other art forms, Armenian literature has been significantly influenced by religion. As in Europe, medieval Armenia was home to an important class of monks who spent much of their time writing, translating, and preserving works of literature. From the fifth to the tenth centuries, most Armenian poetry was written within the walls of monasteries. One of Armenia's literary pioneers was the founder of the Armenian alphabet, the monk Mesrop Mashdotz, who wrote *sharakans,* short poems meant to be chanted during church services. Many later Armenian poets followed the rhythm and structure of the *sharakans.* But the tenth-century poets Krikor Naregatsi and Nerses Shnorali carried their poetry away from the confines of religion, writing in a freer, more lyrical style that found acceptance among ordinary readers.

Later, one of the most popular Armenian poets, Sayat Nova, adopted words and phrases from other languages, including Turkish, Persian, and Kurdish. By using common expressions from these tongues, Sayat Nova found an audience well beyond speakers of the Armenian language. Sayat Nova continues to be popular and to this day, Armenians still enjoy recitals of his works in the capital. Small touring groups provide free weekend recitals in Armenian cities, engaging in competitions and inviting their audiences to participate.

Armenian literature enjoyed a heyday in the nineteenth century. In 1840, the first Armenian novel was written by Khachatur Abovian. Novelist Raffi and poet Ghevond Alishan brought major influences from the West and the East, respectively, and established the new traditions of epic poetry and the novel. Poet Hovhanness Toumanian drew from Armenian folklore, while the anguished Siamanto, Daniel Varoujan, was a poet of country life. Armenia's great political poet and writer was Mikayel Nalbandian.

During the Soviet period, Armenian writing took a new direction. Forced to conform to the state's regulation of topics and literary styles, most Soviet-era writers limited their writing to topics outside of politics. Some poets of this period, however, including Baruir Sevag and Yeghishe Charents, tested the limits on their art with lyrics that expressed both cynicism and rebellion.

Since independence, Armenian literature has been limited to new translations of Armenian poets, such as Sayat Nova, from Armenian into English. These translations, largely financed by Armenians in other parts of the world, have been designed for an Armenian audience in the United States and Europe. Sadly, many of Armenia's most famous modern singers, musicians, and actors have emigrated for more promising opportunities in Russia and the West. Over the past ten years, these artists have been hard-pressed to earn a livable wage within Armenia, and their emigration has left a void in Armenian culture that will be difficult for those who remain to fill.

Culture in Azerbaijan

The arts have played a prominent role in Azeri society throughout the nation's history. Literature, in the form of short stories and poetry, historically reached a wide audience, and Azerbaijan is well known for its intricate textile art, and especially for carpets that display Islamic calligraphy and religious design.

As is the case elsewhere, Azeri literature affected the nation's language. The people of Azerbaijan speak a language that is closely related to Anatolian Turkish. Modern Azerbaijani owes a great debt to the work of Mirza Muhammad Ali Kazembeck, who wrote a series of grammar textbooks in the 1830s and 1840s. Kazembeck simplified the language and provided it with a uniform set of rules and practices. His works established Azerbaijani as a distinct member of the Turkic language family.

A popular playwright, Mirza Akhundzade, also helped develop the Azerbaijani language during the 1830s. His popular plays, written in colloquial Azerbaijani, served as a new model for writers and students. The plays commonly appeared in newspapers, a medium that was spreading culture and the arts to the mass of ordinary readers who could not afford books. Newspapers were economical, and their simplified versions of stories and plays made the works of Akhundzade and others appealing to many people. Nowadays, several modern Baku theaters, sponsored by Western oil companies currently active in Azerbaijan, stage the plays of Akhundzade. Such foreign investment in Azeri culture has made the work of Akhundzade and many others accessible and affordable to the average Azeri.

Azeri Literature and Music

Azerbaijani writing enjoyed a golden age during the eleventh century, a literary epoch highlighted by the religious text *Avesta* and a collection of oral recitations, or *dastans*, such as *The Book of Dede Korkut* and *Koroglu*. Abdul Hasan Shirvani wrote on the subject of astronomy in the eleventh or twelfth century. *Khamseh* is a long set of complex romantic poems written in Persian by the twelfth-century poet Nezami Ganjavi. The poetry and prose of Fuzuli (1494–1556) also holds a prominent place in Azerbaijani literature. Fuzuli's most famous works were the poem "Laila and Majnun," the popular *Book of Complaints*, and *To the Heights of Conviction*, a work of philosophy.

During the ninteenth century, many promising Azeri students studied at universities in Europe, Russia, and Turkey. They returned with foreign ideas and styles that renewed and invigorated Azerbaijani culture. According to historian Audrey Altstadt, these new cultural leaders included "an educated and

RELIGION IN THE TRANSCAUCASUS

Founded as an atheistic state, the Soviet Union did what it could to suppress religion and convince the people to place their faith in public institutions founded on Communist principles. However, throughout the nation and in the Transcaucaus in particular, the effort failed. As one noted expert in the region, Ronald Grigor Suny, wrote in *Transcaucasia: Nationalism and Social Change:*

> Though religion played far less central a role in the life of people than it had in the pre-Soviet period, the press frequently carried reports of religious ceremonies, ostentatious feasting, funerals that continued for days.... In Azerbaijan a 1982–83 poll showed that most Azerbaijanis observe both Soviet and Islamic marriage and funeral customs. Young people between the ages of 16 and 20 were even more likely to invite a mullah or priest to a funeral (88.6 percent) than the oldest group surveyed, those over sixty (79.2 percent).... For all three major nationalities in the Transcaucasus, and for many of the smaller ones as well, national culture was nearly indivisible from their historical religious self-definition. Yet it was precisely the weeding out of religious elements within these cultures that the Soviet government was most anxious to achieve.

Despite the suppression of religion by the Soviet government, many Transcaucasians continued to observe religious customs in their funerals and weddings.

An Azeri folk dancer prepares for a performance. Music and dance continue to play a pivotal role in Azerbaijani culture.

active group of writers, composers, dramatists, journalists, teachers, engineers and medical doctors."[24] Some of the most famous of these new cultural leaders included Nariman Narimanov, a playwright, teacher, and doctor; the writer and composer Uzeir Hajibeyli; and Memed Hasan Hajinskii, a noted engineer and writer. These men promoted the arts in the schools of higher education in Azerbaijan.

Opera, ballet, and theater flourished in Azerbaijan in the nineteenth and twentieth centuries. Classical Azerbaijani music drew heavily on literary works. Musical compositions by traditional poet-singers, called *ashrugs*, used the *kobuz*, a stringed instrument, to accompany recitations of ancient verse. The folk music commonly heard in Azerbaijani villages alternated vocal and instrumental segments.

Azeri operas were the first to incorporate Islamic themes in their music and stories. The brothers Uzeir and Jeyhun Hajibeyli contributed to a rich tradition of theater and opera in the Azeri language. Some of their most famous satiric operas are still performed in the main opera house in Baku, where composer Jeyhun Hajibeyli remains popular for his satire of traditional practices and cultural taboos. For example, Hajibeyli harshly criticized traditional arranged marriages in two comedic operas, *Arshin Mal Alan* and *Meshtibad*. *Arshin Mal Alan* features a young man pretending to be a tailor in order to approach a young woman. (Hajibeyli shocked conservative Muslim audiences by actually using a woman, an Azerbaijani actress trained in Italy, to play the role of the young man's beloved.)

Meshtibad describes a young couple in love and a strict father, who intends on marrying his daughter to a middle-aged, alcoholic merchant. In one scene, the young man substitutes himself for the veiled bride during the wedding ceremony, a ruse that leads to all sorts of hilarious confusion.

GEORGIAN CULTURE

As in Azerbaijan and Armenia, traditional Georgian culture was closely associated with religious faith and ritual. The Christian religion was brought to Georgia by missionaries sent by the Roman emperor Constantine in the fourth century, and historians believe that the Bible was translated into Georgian as early as the fifth century. Georgians remained within the church even as Islamic armies invaded and nearly surrounded them in later centuries.

Georgian visual arts, particularly architecture, often find expression through the church. The distinctive circular design of Georgian church domes, or cupolas, is one example. The domed church evolved into many distinct forms over the centuries. "Free-cross" churches have different cruciform layouts, that is, floor plans that resemble a cross. The *idleti* variety has a four-square area at the end of the north, south, and west ends of the cross, and a horseshoe shape at the eastern end. Yet another form, the *tetraconch*, resembles a four-leaf clover when viewed from above. The most famous tetraconch church, the seventh-century Church of Dzhvari, served as a model for many later Georgian architects. But in Georgia, architecture was not the only art form that found expression in churches.

Stoneworkers and sculptors also held a place of high regard among all Georgian artists. Exterior decoration matched the detail and skill of interior design. Representations of animals, botanical forms, and abstract geometric designs embellished walls, pillars, and portals.

Impressive frescoes and holy icons have decorated Georgian church interiors for centuries. Some religious paintings covered entire walls and ceilings; Georgian painters gained a wide reputation for these murals.

But Georgia's sculptors also expressed themselves in secular venues. One of the most famous modern Georgian sculptors, Elguja Amasukheli, gained international fame for the outstanding monuments and statues he designed for the Georgian capital. Amasukheli's work can be seen as far away as the museums and galleries of France, Germany, Italy, and Canada.

The Church of Dzhvari (pictured) in Georgia is the most famous example of a tetraconch church.

Metalworking also has a long history in Georgia. The Transcaucasus region offered plentiful natural resources for those who worked in silver, bronze, and gold. Georgians learned how to forge, solder, stamp, and emboss metal thousands of years ago, and skilled smiths also created delicately filigreed jewelry and pendants. Georgians even applied their metalworking skill to their literature—some book covers that have survived medieval times are beautifully decorated in silver and gold.

MUSIC AND LITERATURE

Georgian folk music is famous for its complex, three-part multiphonic harmonies. But each region of the country has its own distinct performing style, in music as well as dance. Georgian folksongs are still sung today at ceremonial dinners, where guests enjoy the music and the familiar rituals of improvised toasts. Ninteenth-century Georgian composers, such as Paliashvili, Balanchivadze, and Arakishvili began writing operas in the European style. As was happening throughout western Europe, conservatories were founded, and symphony orchestras and chamber groups were formed. But the real musical treasure of Georgia remained its fascinating and complex folk music. (So distinctive is this art form that a recording of a well-known Georgian song, "Chakrulo," was selected as one of the works carried aboard the NASA deep-space probe, *Voyager*, designed in part to communicate the essence of humanity to whatever higher life forms might exist in distant galaxies.)

Georgia's literature began with ancient ballads and heroic epics passed down orally by performers over the centuries. A Greek writer, Apollonius Rhodius, describes the oldest of these, the legend of Amirani, in the third century B.C. The oldest surviving folk poems date from the fifth century. For many years after the establishment of Christianity in Georgia, Georgian writers produced religious works, such as the lives of the saints and translations of the Bible. But secular literature flourished in the twelfth century, when the chivalrous adventure *Amiran-Darejaniani* was written by Mose Khoneli.

One of the most famous achievements of Georgian literature is *The Knight in the Panther's Skin*, an epic historical poem by Shota Rustaveli. Written in the late twelfth century, the poem is a lyrical adventure story of three heroes. Georgians also can boast of several national epics, among them the *Baramiani* and the *Rostomiani*, both written by Sarg of Thmogvi. Georgian

THE GREAT CHESS TRADITION OF GEORGIA

The game of chess has a long history in Georgia and is still popular today. Although some believe the Persians brought chess to Georgia, others trace its origins to Indian merchants traveling the Silk Road between Asia and Europe. The Chess House in Tbilisi, which opened in 1973, became a national education and tournament center and has hosted many championship matches.

Georgian families traditionally gave their daughters a copy of Rustaveli's epic poem *The Knight in Panther's Skin*, along with a chess set, as wedding presents. The most famous and successful modern Georgian chess players have been women. Nona Gaprindashvili became Women's World Champion in 1962 and held the title for sixteen years, to be replaced in 1978 by another Georgian, Maya Chiburdanidze. The title of the Women's World Champion belonged to Georgians for thirty years, from 1962 until 1991; afterward a team of Georgian women (M. Chiburdanidze, N. Gaprindashvili, N. Ioseliani, K. Arakhamia, and N. Gurieli) won the Women's Chess Olympiad in 1992, 1994, and 1996.

literature also features popular plays and comedies, often with added musical scores to entertain audiences.

THE UNCERTAIN FUTURE

The desperate economic situation of the post-Soviet era is posing a serious challenge to the arts and culture in the Transcaucasus. The new governments have been hard-pressed to fund arts projects, while few citizens can afford tickets to the opera, to theater performances, to art galleries, or to concerts. Economic problems have taken a toll on education as well. Art and music students continue to enter national conservatories, but it has become increasingly difficult for such academies to hire instructors, due to lack of money.

Independence for the nations of the Transcaucasus has been hard—harder than many people at first believed it would be. But someday, the nations of the Transcaucasus will regain their financial and social balance. The people will adapt themselves to their new economy and way of life, and workers and families will enjoy a better standard of living and more leisure time. When this happens, the writers, artists, and musicians of the Transcaucasus likely will see their audiences and popular interest grow, and the cultural life of the Transcaucasus will revive.

EPILOGUE

REBUILDING THE TRANSCAUCASUS

Just as the geography of the Transcaucasus protected it from most invaders, so too did the terrain limit and define trade and commerce. The Armenians, Georgians, and Azerbaijanis shared a common role in developing and cornering a part of the trade passing through the region. Acting as middlemen, nearly all elements of society had something to do with trade, and for more than two millenia the people of the Transcaucasus have earned a reputation as skillful traders and commercial brokers.

With limited access to the sea, the people of the Transcaucasus had to depend on slower, and more expensive, overland trade. Traditionally, nonperishable goods such as spices, precious metals, handicrafts, and woven textiles such as rugs and tapestries made up the bulk of the region's trade goods. But the importance of trade to the people of the Transcaucasus meant that prosperity depended on their relations with neighboring powers.

When the Transcaucasus was part of the Soviet Union, the government in Moscow, the Soviet capital, enforced economic cooperation among the three republics. On winning their independence, the new governments of the Transcaucasus had to overcome the lingering effects of many years of Soviet control, which oriented their industries and resources to meet the needs of a centrally planned economy. While Soviet planners once subsidized obsolete industries for the sake of full employment, reforms carried out during the 1990s brought about a free-market economy, in which prices and wages rise and fall according to supply and demand. Left on their own, the nations of the Transcaucasus now must buy and sell in the world market and compete with other countries boasting the latest technology and fully modernized industries.

At the same time, the Transcaucasus republics are facing social problems such as a lack of medical care, struggling economies, and a relatively high infant mortality rate. A rising rate of unemployment has affected nearly every family in the region, and the poor economic conditions have forced thousands of Armenians, Azerbaijanis, and Georgians to emigrate. In an underpopulated nation such as Armenia, the smallest of all the former Soviet republics, this emigration poses a very serious challenge, especially since most of those who leave are precisely the educated, skilled workers most needed in helping their country rebuild.

The need for cooperation in the Transcaucasus has been demonstrated throughout the region's history and remains the most serious challenge for these countries today. Yet conflict over territory has brought trade embargos and blockades, affecting these nations' ability to export their goods. There have been isolated outbreaks of violence, urban rioting, and outright war.

In an effort to increase cooperation between the nations of the Transcaucasus, secretary of state Colin Powell met with leaders of the Transcaucasus republics on April 3, 2001.

Above all, then, the nations of the Transcaucasus need to settle their many conflicts and disputes over territory. Only when they reach some kind of agreement over their borders will the governments of the Transcaucasus be able to attract foreign investment and rebuild crumbling roads, railroads, pipelines, and other infrastructure. Whether the leaders of the Transcaucasus see that the economic needs of their people are more important than the conflicts of the past will define the future for this vital region.

FACTS ABOUT
THE TRANSCAUCASUS

REPUBLIC OF ARMENIA

Total area:
29,800 sq. km; slightly larger than Maryland

Bordering states:
Azerbaijan (east)
Naxçivan (south)
Georgia
Iran
Turkey

Population:
3.6 million
68% urban
110.5 persons/sq. km

Ethnic composition:
93.3% Armenian, 1.7% Kurdish, 1.5% Russian, 3.5% Assyrian, Greek,
other

REPUBLIC OF GEORGIA

Total area:
69,700 sq. km; slightly larger than South Carolina

Bordering states:
Armenia
Azerbaijan
Russia
Turkey

Population:
5.57 million
56% urban
78 persons/sq. km

Ethnic composition:

69% Georgian, 9% Armenian, 6% Russian, 6% Ajarian, 5% Azerbaijani,
3% Ossetian, 2% Abkhazian

Georgia includes the autonomous republics of Abkhazia and Ajaria
and the South Ossetian Autonomous Region.

REPUBLIC OF AZERBAIJAN

Total area:

81,800 sq. km; slightly smaller than Maine

Bordering states:

Armenia (west)

Armenia (southwest)

Georgia

Iran (south)

Iran (southwest)

Russia

Turkey

Population:

7.3 million

54% urban

89 persons/sq. km

Ethnic composition:

71% Azerbaijani, 11% Talysh, 6% Russian, 4% Lezgin, 3% Dagestani,
3% Kurdish

The autonomous republic of Naxçivan (pop. 350,000; 5,500 sq. km)
was placed under Azerbaijani administration in the early 1920s.

NOTES

CHAPTER 1: MOUNTAINS AND CROSSROADS

1. Robert Bedrosian, "Eastern Asia Minor and the Caucasus in Ancient Mythologies," http://www.virtualscape.com/rbedrosian/mythint.htm.

2. Suzanne Goldenberg, *Pride of Small Nations: The Caucasus and Post-Soviet Disorder*. London: Zed Books, 1994, p. 10

3. Richard Clogg, "Turmoil in Transcaucasia," *World Today*, January 1994, p. 3.

CHAPTER 2: THE CONQUESTS OF THE TRANSCAUCASUS

4. Quoted in "The Fire-Temple at Baku," in Sylvia Volk, "The Page of Myths," http://www.ucalgary.ca/~chilton/Baku.htm.

5. Shireen T. Hunter, *The Transcaucasus in Transition: Nation-Building and Conflict*. Washington, D.C.: Center for Strategic and International Studies, 1994, p. 10.

6. Audrey L. Altstadt, *The Azerbaijani Turks: Power and Identity Under Russian Rule*. Stanford, CA: Hoover Institution Press, 1992, p. 70.

7. Alexandre Benningsen and S. Enders Winbush, *Muslims of the Soviet Empire*. Bloomington: Indiana University Press, 1986, p. 213.

8. Goldenberg, *Pride of Small Nations*, p. 28.

9. Tadeusz Swietochowski, *Russian Azerbaijan 1905–1920: The Shaping of a National Identity in a Muslim Community*. London: Cambridge University Press, 1985, p. 21.

10. Anahide Ter Minassian, "The Revolution of 1905 in Transcaucasia," *Armenian Review*, vol. 42, no. 2, Summer 1989, p. 14.

11. Christopher Walker, *Armenia and Karabagh: The Struggle for Unity*. London: Minority Rights Publications, 1991, p. 32.

CHAPTER 3: THE SOVIET ERA

12. Levon Chorbajian, Patrick Donabedian, and Claude Mutafian, *The Caucasian Knot: The History and Geopolitics of Nagorno-Karabagh.* London: Zed Books, 1994, p. 19.

13. William E. Odom and Robert Dujarric, *Commonwealth or Empire: Russia, Central Asia, and the Transcaucasus.* Indianapolis: Hudson Institute Press, 1995, p. 9.

14. Jean Radvanyi, "Observations on Independence and Statehood in Transcaucasia," *Post-Soviet Geography,* vol. 35, March 1994, p. 179.

15. Elizabeth Fuller, "The Transcaucasus," *Radio Free Europe/Radio Liberty Research Report,* vol. 3, no. 16, April 22, 1994, p. 40.

16. Ronald Wixman, "Ethnic Nationalism in the Caucasus," *Nationalities Papers,* 1990, p. 142.

CHAPTER 4: THE HARD ROAD TO INDEPENDENCE

17. Quoted in Hunter, *The Transcaucasus in Transition,* p. 1.

18. Joseph R. Masih and Robert O. Krikorian, *Armenia at the Crossroads.* Amsterdam: Harwood Publishing, 1999, p. 47.

19. Quoted in Drastamat Isaryan, "Armenia: Until There Are No More Trees," *Bulletin of Atomic Scientists,* January/February 1994, vol. 50, no. 1, p. 12.

20. Elizabeth Fuller, "The Transcaucasus: Real Independence Remains Elusive," *Radio Free Europe/Radio Liberty Research Report,* January 3, 1992, p. 46.

21. Stephen Brook, *Claws of the Crab: Georgia and Armenia in Crisis.* London: Sinclair-Stevenson, 1992, p. 301.

CHAPTER 5: EVERY DAY IS A STRUGGLE

22. Janin Friend, "Abandoning a Sinking Country," *Business Week,* November 6, 2000, p. 20.

23. Quoted in Friend, "Abandoning a Sinking Country," p. 20.

CHAPTER 6: THE ART AND LITERATURE OF THE TRANSCAUCASUS

24. Altstadt, *The Azerbaijani Turks,* p. 50.

CHRONOLOGY

B.C.

66
Romans complete conquest of Caucasus Mountains region, including Georgian kingdom of Kartli-Iberia.

30
Romans conquer Armenian Empire.

A.D.

100–300
Romans annex Azerbaijan.

ca. 600
Four centuries of Arab control of Azerbaijan begin, introducing Islam in seventh century.

645
Arabs capture Tbilisi.

653
Byzantine Empire cedes Armenia to Arabs.

813
Armenian prince Ashot I begins one thousand years of rule in Georgia by Bagratid dynasty.

Eleventh–fourteenth centuries

Byzantine Greeks invade Armenia from west, Seljuk Turks from east; Turkish groups wrest political control of Azerbaijan from Arabs, introducing Turkish language and culture.

1099–1125
David IV the Builder establishes expanded Georgian Empire and begins golden age of Georgia.

1000–late 1200s
Golden age of Azerbaijani literature and architecture.

1375
Cilician Armenia conquered by Mamluk Turks.

1386
Timur (Tamerlane) sacks Tbilisi, ending Georgian Empire.

Fifteenth century

Most of modern Armenia, Azerbaijan, and Georgia become
part of Ottoman Empire.

1553
Ottoman Turks and Persians divide Georgia between them.

ca. 1700
Russia begins moving into northern Azerbaijan as Persian
Empire weakens.

1801
After Herekle II's appeal for aid, Russian empire abolishes
Bagratid dynasty and begins annexation of Georgia.

1813
Treaty of Gulistan officially divides Azerbaijan into Russian
(northern) and Persian (southern) spheres.

1828
Treaty of Turkmanchay awards Naxçivan and area around
Yerevan to Russia, strengthening Russian control of Transcauc-
asus and beginning period of modernization and stability.

1872
Oil industry established around Baku, beginning rapid expansion.

1895
Massacre of three hundred thousand Armenian subjects by
Ottoman Turks.

1905
Clashes erupt in Azerbaijan between local Azerbaijanis and
Armenian residents of the country; become known as the
Armeno-Tatar conflict.

1908
Young Turks take over government of Ottoman Empire
with reform agenda, supported by Armenian population.

1915
Young Turks launch genocide of 1.5 million Armenians; most survivors leave eastern Anatolia.

1917
Armenia, Azerbaijan, and Georgia form independent Transcaucasian federation. Czar Nicholas II abdicates Russian throne; Bolsheviks take power in Russia.

1918
Independent Armenian, Azerbaijani, and Georgian states emerge from defeat of Ottoman Empire in World War I.

1920
Red Army invades Azerbaijan and forces Armenia to accept Communist-dominated government.

1921
Red Army invades Georgia.

1922
Transcaucasian Federated Soviet Socialist Republic combines Armenia, Azerbaijan, and Georgia as single republic within Soviet Union.

1936
Armenia, Azerbaijan, and Georgia become separate republics within Soviet Union.

1969
Geidar Aliyev named head of Azerbaijani Communist Party.

ca. 1970
Zviad Gamsakhurdia begins organizing dissident Georgian nationalists.

1978
Mass demonstrations prevent Moscow from making Russian an official language of Georgia.

1985
Eduard Shevardnadze named minister of foreign affairs of Soviet Union and leaves post as first secretary of Georgian Communist Party.

Late 1980s
Mikhail S. Gorbachev initiates policies of glasnost and perestroika throughout Soviet Union.

1988
Armenian nationalist movement launched with Nagorno-Karabakh, environmental concerns as core issues; Nagorno-Karabakh government votes to unify with Armenia; riots and mob violence in Azerbaijani city of Sumgait kill local Armenians; devastating earthquake hits the northern districts of Armenia in December.

1989
Azerbaijan imposes full blockade of Armenia; all transport routes and energy pipelines are cut. Azerbaijani blockade also cuts off Nagorno-Karabakh from any direct contact with Armenia. Turkey helps Azerbaijan by maintaining blockade of Armenia's western border.

1990
January
Moscow dispatches troops to Azerbaijan after mob violence targets Armenian population living in Baku; local Armenians forced to flee to safety in Armenia.

August
Armenia declares independent statehood; Abkhazia declares independence from Georgia.

1991
January
Georgian forces invade South Ossetia to put down ethnic Ossetians' attempt to unite with neighboring North Ossetia, effectively breaking away from Georgian control; fighting continues for nearly a year until reaching a stalemate.

April
Following the favorable results of a national referendum, the Georgian parliament declares Georgian independence from the Soviet Union.

May
Zviad Gamsakhurdia becomes first president of Georgia, elected directly in multiparty election.

September
Armenian voters approve national independence; Azerbaijan declares independence from Soviet Union; former Communist leader Ayaz Mutalibov wins Azerbaijani presidential election in a one-candidate contest.

October
Nationalist leader and parliamentary chairman Levon Ter
Petrosian elected president of Armenia.

December
Armenians in Nagorno-Karabakh declare independent state
as fighting there continues; Soviet Union officially dissolved.

1992
January
Gamsakhurdia driven from Georgia into exile by opposition
forces.

March
Shevardnadze forms new government in Georgia.

June
Nationalist leader of the Azerbaijani Popular Front Abulfez
Elchibey elected president of Azerbaijan; Azerbaijani mili-
tary attack on Nagorno-Karabakh is launched.

June
As rebel units of the Azerbaijani military march on Baku attempting to overthrow the government of Elchibey in Azerbaijan, former Soviet-era official Geidar Aliyev returns to power.

1993
October
Georgian president leads Georgia to join Commonwealth of
Independent States, thus gaining Russian military support;
Geidar Aliyev elected president of Azerbaijan.

SUGGESTIONS FOR FURTHER READING

Stephen Brook, *Claws of the Crab: Georgia and Armenia in Crisis.* London: Sinclair-Stevenson, 1992. A journalist visits Tbilisi, Yerevan, and other locations as the Soviet Union collapses and as Georgia and Armenia struggle to establish independent states.

Levon Chorbajian, Patrick Donabedian, and Claude Mutafian, *The Caucasian Knot: The History and Geopolitics of Nagorno-Karabagh.* London: Zed Books, 1994. Review of the history of Nagorno-Karabakh and the modern dispute over the region, an Armenian enclave within Azerbaijan.

Darra Goldstein and Niko Pirosmani, *The Georgian Feast: The Vibrant Culture and Savory Food of the Republic of Georgia.* Berkeley and Los Angeles: University of California Press, 1999. Georgian legends, culture, geography, history, and food.

Thomas Goltz, *Azerbaijan Diary: A Rogue Reporter's Adventures in an Oil-Rich, War-Torn, Post-Soviet Republic.* Armonk, NY: M. E. Sharpe, 1998. A freelance reporter detours into Azerbaijan's capital of Baku and, sensing a good story, decides to stay—for six years—and report on the country's ethnic, religious, and political turmoil.

Philip Marsden, *The Crossing Place: A Journey Among the Armenians.* New York: Kondasha International, 1995. An English journalist journeys through the modern Armenian community, traveling through seventeen countries and recounting the effects of Armenia's turbulent ancient and modern history.

Tadeusz Swietochowski, *Russia and Azerbaijan: A Borderland in Transition.* New York: Columbia University Press, 1995. Study of Azerbaijan's history in the late Russian and Soviet empires and the rivalry between Russians and Iranians over influence in the Transcaucasus.

Pierre Verluis and Levon Chorbajian, *Armenia in Crisis: The 1988 Earthquake.* Detroit: Wayne State University Press, 1995. Documentary study of the devastating 1988 earthquake, detailing the human and physical damage and asserting that the resulting political controversy led to the final collapse of the Soviet Union.

WORKS CONSULTED

BOOKS

Audrey L. Altstadt, *The Azerbaijani Turks: Power and Identity Under Russian Rule.* Stanford, CA: Hoover Institution Press, 1992. Using Russian and Azerbaijani newspapers, journals, and magazines, the author gives the Azerbaijani perspective on the tumultuous 200-year relationship between Azerbaijan and Russia, and describes the efforts by Azerbaijanis to protect their heritage and culture through native-language education and the arts.

Nadia Diuk and Adrian Karatnycky, *New Nations Rising: The Fall of the Soviets and the Challenge of Independence.* New York: John Wiley & Sons, 1993. A description of the powerful wave of nationalism that overcame the Soviet republics, including the three nations of the Transcaucasus, in the 1980s and 1990s and how that nationalism is shaping the current politics within those former republics.

Carolyn McGiffert Ekedahl and Melvin A. Goodman, *The Wars of Eduard Shevardnadze.* University Park: Pennsylvania State University Press, 1997. A CIA public communications chief and a war studies professor at the National War College study the rise of Eduard Shevardnadze, his career as Soviet foreign minister, his role in the last years of the Cold War, and his return to Georgia after the Soviet collapse.

Suzanne Goldenberg, *Pride of Small Nations: The Caucasus and Post-Soviet Disorder.* London: Zed Books, 1994. Overview of the Soviet collapse as it affected the Transcaucasus region, including chapters on the war in Nagorno-Karabakh and the breakaway republics of Georgia.

Edmund Herzig, *The New Caucasus: Armenia, Azerbaijan and Georgia.* London: RIIA, 1999. An analysis of the Transcaucasus nations five years after independence, focusing on political stability and economic development.

Shireen T. Hunter, *Transcaucasus in Transition: Nation-Building and Conflict.* Washington, D.C.: Center for Strategic and International Studies, 1994. A think-tank project on the Transcaucasus, introducing the region's history, from ancient times to independence, and analysis of the impact of economic and military strategy of the larger and more powerful neighbors.

David Remnick, *Lenin's Tomb: The Last Days of the Soviet Empire*. New York: Random House, 1993. A detailed, street-level description of events in the Soviet Union that led up to the end of the Soviet Union, focusing on the corruption and inefficiency that plagued the economy and the lives of ordinary people.

Ronald Grigor Suny, *Transcaucasia: Nationalism and Social Change*. Ann Arbor: University of Michigan Press, 1996. A leading scholar and expert on the Transcaucasus region describes the social and political changes that took place in the region since the 1960s and through the early 1990s.

PERIODICALS

Richard Clogg, "Turmoil in Transcaucasia," *World Today*, January 1994.

Economist, "What Next?," November 11, 2000.

Janin Friend, "Abandoning a Sinking Country," *Business Week*, November 6, 2000.

Maarten A. Gischler, "Beautifying the Bay: New Environmental Project Launched," *Azerbaijan International*, Summer 2000, http://www.azer.com/aiweb/categories/magazine.

Paul Glasris, "Armenia's History, Turkey's Dilemma," *Washington Post*, March 11, 2001.

Edmund M. Herzig, "Armenians," in Graham Smith, ed., *The Nationalities Question in the Soviet Union*. London: Longman, 1990.

Susanna Petrosian, "Armenia's Nuclear Dilemma," *Institute for War and Peace Reporting*, March 9, 2001, http://iwpr.vs4.cerbernet.co.uk.

Michael Specter, "Rainy Days in Georgia," *New Yorker*, December 18, 2000.

Anahide Ter Minassian, "The Revolution of 1905 in Transcaucasia," *Armenian Review* vol. 42, no. 2, Summer 1989.

WEBSITES

Robert Bedrosian, "Eastern Asia Minor and the Caucasus in Ancient Mythologies," http://www.virtualscape.com/rbedrosian/mythint.htm.

"The Fire-Temple at Baku," in Sylvia Volk, "The Page of Myths," http://www.ucalgary.ca/~chilton/Baku.htm.

"Georgian Culture," http://www.sangha.net/countries/Georgia/culture.htm.

ADDITIONAL WORKS CONSULTED

BOOKS

Alexandre Benningsen and S. Enders Winbush, *Muslims of the Soviet Empire*. Bloomington: Indiana University Press, 1986.

Joseph R. Masih and Robert O. Krikorian, *Armenia at the Crossroads*. Amsterdam: Harwood Publishing, 1999.

William E. Odom and Robert Dujarric, *Commonwealth or Empire: Russia, Central Asia, and the Transcaucasus*. Indianapolis: Hudson Institute Press, 1995.

Tadeusz Swietochowski, *Russian Azerbaijan 1905–1920: The Shaping of a National Identity in a Muslim Community*. London: Cambridge University Press, 1985.

Christopher Walker, *Armenia and Karabagh: The Struggle for Unity*. London: Minority Rights Publications, 1991.

PERIODICALS

Elizabeth Fuller, "The Transcaucasus," *Radio Free Europe/Radio Liberty Research Report*, vol. 3, no. 16, April 22, 1994.

———, "The Transcaucasus: Real Independence Remains Elusive," *Radio Free Europe/Radio Liberty Research Report*, January 3, 1992.

Drastamat Isaryan, "Armenia: Until There Are No More Trees," *Bulletin of Atomic Scientists*, January/February 1994, vol. 50, no. 1.

Jean Radvanyi, "Observations on Independence and Statehood in Transcaucasia," *Post-Soviet Geography*, vol. 35, March 1994.

Ronald Wixman, "Ethnic Nationalism in the Caucasus," *Nationalities Papers*, 1990.

INDEX

Picture Credits

ABOUT THE AUTHOR

Tom Streissguth has written more than 30 books of non-fiction for young readers, from *Life Among the Vikings* to *Utopian Visionaries; Lewis and Clark; Wounded Knee: The End of the Plains Indian Wars;* and the award-winning *Hustlers and Hoaxers.* He has written or collaborated on dozens of geography books as well as biographies and descriptive histories. His interests include music, languages, and travel. He has also co-founded a private language school, "Learn French!", which hosts summer tours each year in Europe. He lives in Florida with his wife and two daughters.